As he opened the door, he started back in surprise. "Fore God," he said "did I not know, I should think it Lord Carthew in life again"

HEARTS AND
THE HIGHWAY

A ROMANCE OF THE ROAD

*First set forth by Lady Katharine Clanranald and Sir
Hugh Richmond and now transcribed by
Cyrus Townsend Brady*

Author of " The Island of Regeneration," "The
Better Man," etc.

WITH FOUR ILLUSTRATIONS
BY F. C. YOHN

A. L. BURT COMPANY

PUBLISHERS   NEW YORK

Dedicated to

MRS. HARRIETTE ROSCOE ELLARD

AND HER DEVOTED ASSOCIATES
IN THE LIVELIEST AND MOST ENTHUSIASTIC
WOMAN'S AUXILIARY SOCIETY THAT I KNOW

PREFACE

THIS story is exactly what it purports to be, a romance, as the reader who cares to follow the Highway with the Hero and Heroine whose adventures thereon are hereafter set forth will see. It makes no pretence at being an historical novel, and yet, perhaps, it is only fair to the Manes of Lady Grizel Ogilby to point out that she herself once played a dashing rôle, somewhat like that attributed to Lady Katharine Clanranald, in a similar emergency in Scottish history and at a similar crisis in the family fortunes. I am just a little tired, for the nonce, of the problem story, and I have turned to this with a keen relish in which I humbly trust the reader will share. Variety is the life of literature: if I confined myself to one kind of books, or to one kind of sermons, I should be a dead author and a dead preacher as well.

The relaxations of life are not to be found in idleness, but in doing things that are different. It is a far cry from *The Island of Regeneration* to *The Better Man* and from *The Better Man*

to *Hearts and the Highway.* And it will be a
farther cry, perhaps, to the next story! Here's
hoping that each may find a place and welcome in
some gracious reader's heart.

CYRUS TOWNSEND BRADY.

St. George's Rectory, Kansas City, Mo.,
New Year's Day, 1911.

CONTENTS

BOOK I

THE WINNING OF A HUSBAND

*As Set Forth by the Lady of the Quest,
with a Necessary Interlude by the
Gentleman in Person*

CHAPTER I

———

BOOK II

THE KEEPING OF A WIFE

*As Described by the Gentleman Who Did It,
with an Incidental Digression by
the Lady Herself*

BOOK I

THE WINNING OF A HUSBAND

*As set forth by the Lady of the Quest,
with a necessary Interlude by the
Gentleman in Person*

Chapter

I

*In which I, Lady Katharine Clanranald, come to
a desperate but manly Resolution*

"TIME," said the councillor gravely, "is all
that we lack."

"And money, sir," I added most disconsolately.

"True," was the somewhat amused answer of
the grim old attorney. "The King hath very
pressing need of money ever, and with the Stuart
disposition there goeth always the itching palm of
Cassius."

"That last need," I commented thoughtfully,
"might be supplied in some measure. There are
the jewels of the Countess, my lady mother, and my
own as well."

"And though the estates be confiscate," returned Master Dunner, "there are certain moneys
in my charge which the justiciaries wot not of, and
which are available for any purpose that will serve
my lord."

"Nay, sir, I would not have you jeopard your own savings," I burst out hurriedly, but he straightway checked me.

"Your ladyship," he said softly, "I am not only an attorney, but in a remote degree I am kin to your family and of your blood. My ancestors followed Clanranald in peace and war. They served him with the sword, I with the pen, 'tis true, but natheless . . ."

"Master Dunner," said I, vastly touched, "you say true, and for the Earl I accept your proffer. Think ye that together we could raise two thousand pounds?"

"With your ladyship's jewels and those of the family which you took precaution to remove before the troopers seized the house, I think with my own poor savings added thereto we might even compass three thousand."

"Scots?" quoth I.

"English, madam."

"'Tis a goodly sum."

"Ay, indeed, but as I had the honour to tell you a moment since, 'tis not money we lack but time."

"Will you explain that to me again, Master Attorney?"

Indeed, I had become quite bewildered by the sudden changes of fortune which had plunged us into this dire misery.

" 'Tis true undoubtedly, madam, that your honoured father did conspire with the Duke of Monmouth or his partisans in Scotland to raise the country in revolt against King Jamie of England, his brother, but there were extenuating circumstances. He was in a manner forced into the enterprise, although his influence and voice were ever raised in restraint. I have prepared a brief here, well attested. Indeed, those of the meaner sort lately executed for treason have cheerfully borne testimony to the Earl's unwillingness, and I have here their depositions. Then, too, there is a recommendation from the Lord Chief Justice, together with a petition signed by various gentlemen praying the King to exercise his royal clemency. If we could get that into his hands backed by that sum of money of which we have spoke, I think there would be no doubt that His Majesty would be pleased to commute the sentence."

He smiled confidently as he concluded.

"Why not send it to him at once then?" I asked rather sharply. "Why delay and waste hours in idle talking?"

" But, your ladyship, I have told you there is no time."

" What mean you? "

" The proceedings in the trial, which was most unduly hurried despite our earnest protests and in which no proper opportunity was given to establish these facts, have been sent to His Majesty in London. On account of the Earl's rank and importance, a royal warrant is required for his execution."

I shuddered at that word, but Master Dunner ran on inflexibly, knowing that I was privy to the worst already.

" The findings of the court were approved with most unseemly haste, and a royal warrant issued which is even now on the way. I have had private advices from a correspondent in London, who hath interest at the Court, that the warrant is being despatched to Edinburgh in the personal custody of Sir Hugh Richmond, an officer of the Royal Army. My messenger coming post-haste hath outstripped him, in part because he hath been obliged to deliver other similar warrants, which hath made his progress slower than one who comes direct."

" But have you not appealed to the Lord Chief

Justice to delay the execution of the warrant until we can communicate with the King?" I asked earnestly.

"Madam, I have, but he is inflexible. He says he hath no power, though with the best will in the world, to stay the execution of a royal warrant."

"But if I should appeal to him?"

"You might as well appeal to the Tolbooth itself."

"Then the case is hopeless?"

"Ay," said the old man gently enough, but with such decision as carried conviction to my sinking heart, "unless by some means the delivery of the warrant can be estopped until we have access to the King."

"Could the messenger be bribed?"

"I fear not. Sir Hugh Richmond is, I am told, a man of independent fortune, a proved soldier, a loyal gentleman."

"I meant not with money, old friend," I replied, smiling at him.

"By Heaven!" answered the advocate, looking me full in the eyes, "if any power could do it, it would be your fair face, my lady, and, given you time and opportunity, I believe you might win any man to your thinking, but here again 'tis impossible."

" But if some one took the warrant from him by force? "

" That would answer," said the advocate, " but who is to do it, madam? It would be high treason in the first place and certain death in the second, and in the present unsettled state of affairs, or rather settled in His Majesty's interest, you could not get a man to lift a hand."

He shook his head gloomily as he finished.

" Could I not? " I replied reflectively. " There are . . ."

And then I stopped.

I had plenty of friends to be sure, and I did not doubt that among them I might find some of sufficient devotion and daring to risk life and fortune to do me this service. Whoever did it, however, would want a reward commensurate with the risk incurred, and with the service rendered. I knew full well what that reward would be. It would be myself, and there was not one among the gay gallants who had paid me court—and who, I doubt not, even now would be at my side, or at my feet, were I not in close hiding, thinking to serve my father better at large than if I were with him in the prison—that I would marry. I was as heart-whole and fancy-free as any maid in Scotland, and would fain remain so; though, if it came to a pinch, I would of course sacrifice my own freedom to any gallant gentleman who would save my good old father's life.

He and I were the last of the Clanranalds. Brother I had had, but he had died two years before, and my mother had long since preceded him. My father and I had been much together at Clanranald House, and I loved him with a devotion, I think, which passed that entertained by most Scottish maids for their fathers. I did not desire to marry anybody. I wanted my father's life saved. I wished to be back again at Clanranald House, the old, sweet, free life flowing on as it did before this bastard Monmouth and his futile ambitions came athwart our path. But that was not to be. Surely some other way might be found to stop the messenger. I strained my wits hard to devise one.

"Madam," said Master Dunner, who had been scrutinising me searchingly as these thoughts ran through my troubled brain, "you know how gladly I would assume the adventure myself, were it not . . ."

He looked down very sadly at his poor clubbed foot and shrunken limb, which had made him an attorney instead of a soldier. He was older than my father, too, and could with difficulty sit a horse.

" I know your will, sir," I interrupted quickly, catching him by the hand, " but that is not to be thought of."

" What, then? "

That he, with all his shrewdness and resource, should ask the question of me, a woman, proved as nothing else the hopelessness of the situation. Yet the question was a sharp spur to my imagination. It seemed to force choice among the men who had paid court to me at Clanranald House in happier days.

" Let me think," replied I, as I passed in rapid review the various young gentlemen of my acquaintance. There was not one of them who was acceptable as a husband in the least degree to me. There must be some other way, and yet . . . I came to a sudden decision.

" I will do it myself," I said boldly with a flash of inspiration.

" You, my lady? " exclaimed the attorney in great amaze.

" Why not I? I can use a small sword with most men of my acquaintance. My father hath given me much of his own skill, and I have never hesitated to cross blades in friendly bout with any of our guests at home. As for other weapons, I have often ranged moor and glen with the Earl; I have brought down a stag and know the use of small arms."

" But you are a woman."

" Can I not for the nonce be a man?" I asked. " What's to hinder, indeed? "

" And do you imagine that, even if you were to attempt to carry out this mad scheme, you could get the better of a tried soldier, an experienced man of the world as rumour accrediteth Sir Hugh Richmond to be?" asked the old man with a slightly ironic touch.

" Since time and the world began, Master Dunner, weak woman, backed by her wit and finesse, hath got the better of strong man," I replied with spirit.

"But you are proposing to approach him as a man."

" I shall be not less a woman for all that," I retorted triumphantly, veering to the other side of the argument, " and being all a woman and half a man . . ."

" Which half, madam? "

" The outward and visible shape thereof," I answered, blushing.

The little attorney laughed grimly.

" 'Fore God," he said, " forgive me, madam, but the thought of you as . . ."

" Master Dunner," said I imperiously, " I am a tall woman as women go "—and I fervently thanked God for the first time in my heart for that fact, heretofore something of a grief to me, since your small women were the fashion then and thereafter—" and I doubt not I will make a braw man enough."

" But your face, madam . . . your hair . . . your voice? "

" I will cut my hair."

" Would you sacrifice . . . ? "

" Peace, man! What is the loss of a few locks, that will grow again, beside my father's head. I will darken my face a bit—indeed, had it been summer instead of spring I should have been brown enough to pass muster—I will wear a wig. and my voice," it was a deep contralto, " will serve. You must get me a suit of clothes, boots, coat, and . . . the other things; a sword, let it be a good one; pistols . . . and, behold! I am transformed."

" And suppose that I fall in with this mad plan of yours, may I ask what further do you intend to assay? "

" Which way rides the messenger? "

" Madam, he comes through Berwick and the road along the shore."

" Will he go to Dalkeith? "

" I think not. Rather by way of Dunbar and Prestonpans."

" When do you expect him? "

" He should be here to-morrow."

" Good! " said I decisively. " 'Tis yet early morning and there is time. Where will he lie to-night? "

" I should think perhaps at Cockenzie. There is an inn there, The Black Douglas, of much repute for travellers, and 'tis an easy journey thence to Edinburgh. He was to stop a night at Berwick, another at Dunbar."

He had the route pat enough, to be sure!

" Think you that your information is to be depended upon? "

" Madam, I believe so."

" I will meet him, then, at Cockenzie. What say you is the name of this famous hostelry? "

" The Black Douglas. But what are your plans then? "

" To act as circumstances may dictate."

" My dear lady," said the old man, coming nearer to me, " forgive my presumption. I have served your race long and well. You have no one left to advise you but me, humble though I am. I must ask to know more of your plans before I consent to aid you."

" And I cannot tell you just exactly what I hope to do."

" But in a general way? "

" In some way or other I shall take from him his despatch-bag, abstract therefrom the warrant for my father. You shall describe it to me so I may identify it easily."

" But . . ."

" Ask me no more! " I cried. " I am resolved upon it. If you will not help me, I shall go myself without your aid."

" Misfortune may befall you."

" What of that? If I am to lose my father, I care not what becomes of me."

" But others care."

" Nay, for no others do I care."

" Madam," he said gravely, " I do think that a bit unkind."

" But for thee," I answered quickly, discerning the trend of his thought. " But because I hold you in honour and you are my last, my only friend, the one being to whom I can appeal, I beg of you question me no further, but give me your aid. The risk is for my father's life and his peril justifieth anything."

" You have won me, madam," said the old man, deeply touched I could see. " Tell me what you wish me to do."

" Procure me clothes suited to my new emprise, a horse—and see that he be a speedy and spirited one, no ambling woman's pad for me, but the best that can be got; money sufficient for any possible wayside need, say a hundred pounds; a sword, an Andrew Ferrara if you can come at one in a hurry; pistols for the holsters; a saddle-bag containing toilet necessaries; a horseman's cloak."

" They shall be here in an hour," said the old man. " I have a suit of your brother's, a riding-suit, which he left at my house when last he visited Edinburgh before his death. 'Tis complete

in all points and will fit you, I doubt not, to per-
fection."

He was a year older than I, but he had been
dead two years and I had had time to catch up
with him.

" There is a sword that belonged to my father
as well. 'Tis a tried blade," said the old man.
" I could not give it into worthier hands, and 'tis
well adapted to your size, for my father was a
man of slight build and did not swing the pon-
derous claymores of your ancestors."

" I am greatly pleased by your willingness to
entrust it to me, Master Dunner. I hope I may
use it as worthily as your father did or any of our
house."

" Madam, you do me proud," said the old
gentleman, bowing like a courtier. " As for the
rest, I will make shift somehow. Would that I
could go with you myself! "

" Would that you could," replied I, "but 'tis
not to be thought of, and there is work for you
to do as well."

" What is that? "

" The ransom money," said I. " It must be
raised and put in bills of exchange upon London.
The papers must be prepared."

" Ay," was the answer, " and if God grant you be successful, they must be despatched to London at once."

" If I am successful, and I must be, I shall take them myself."

" You are your father's daughter! " cried the attorney.

" If you have these things here within the hour, I can reach Cockenzie by nightfall. You should see me back to-morrow. Where shall I meet you? "

" Here," said the advocate. " The woman who keeps the house is devoted to me. No one suspects what this mean dwelling harbours, and 'tis the safest appointment I can give you."

" All's arranged then," said I, giving him my hand.

He bent low over it, and I felt that it had never been pressed by worthier lips than those of the honest advocate.

Chapter
II

Wherein worthy Master Dunner finds My Lord Carthew's Clothes vastly becoming to me as I ride away

MASTER DUNNER was as good as his word. In half an hour there was a huge package, carefully tied up, delivered at the door by one of his clerks. I took it to my own chamber and eagerly cut the lashings. It was a complete suit, of blue and silver. In my distraction, anxiety, and apprehension I had time to think how vastly it became my fair skin and blue eyes and bright hair. I had a wealth of the latter, and I confess, in spite of my brave words, that it was with a considerable pang that I had the woman who kept the house come into the room and, with clumsy, unskilful fingers, crop my long locks with her scissors. Fortunately my hair was curly, and, had it not been that the styles were otherwise, methought as I looked in the glass that the short ringlets were not unbecoming. With the suit were wig to go on one end of me and boots for the other. I was of my brother's height, but my feet were smaller than his; nevertheless, to my great satisfaction, the boots served well.

In my petticoats I was a tall woman; dressed as I found myself presently, I was rather an undersized man, yet not altogether insignificant. My face did look painfully fair: my cheeks pink and white, my upper lip innocent of the faintest suggestion of a moustache; yet, out of some paste from my toilet-table, I did contrive to dull the colour in my cheeks and to impart a brownish cast to my complexion that robbed it of a little of its femininity. My voice, which luckily happened to be a deep contralto, I could manage well enough.

With the suit was a riding-cloak, which I draped about me, and fancied that thus equipped no one could penetrate my disguise. I bore a striking likeness to my brother, too, thus apparelled. It went to my heart, when I looked at myself, to think of my father under sentence of death; alone, childless, save for one poor girl.

I had scarce finished adjusting my wig, clapping my hat upon it, walking up and down the room to accustom myself to the strange garb, when Mas-

ter Dunner was announced. As he opened the
door, he started back in great surprise at what he
saw of me.

" 'Fore God," he said, " did I not know, I
should think it Lord Carthew "—my brother's
courtesy title—" in life again."

His eyes travelled upward and rested upon my
face. He shook his head.

" Save for that burning blush, the imitation is
perfect."

" I think," said I, " that I shall not fly my
colours in that way again. You see "—I sat
down as I spoke and gathered my cloak about
my legs, of which for the first time in my life
I became acutely conscious—" you see, I expect
that all others who look upon me will regard me
as a man, while you know that I am but a woman,
and . . ."

" I see," said the advocate, gravely smiling at
my logic.

" It was foolish of me to blush," said I contritely, " seeing that you are older than my
father."

" I held you in my arms when you were chris-
tened, my lady," remarked the old man simply,
but with feeling.

"I know," I answered.

I rose to my feet and threw back my cloak. I must get accustomed, I thought, to these strange clothes and the world's scrutiny. No better opportunity presented itself for beginning than then and there.

"Hast brought the sword?" I asked, struggling to forget my garb.

For answer he handed it to me, belt and all. The hilt was richly chased and jewelled, but I had seen swords whose whole value consisted in that which rose above the scabbard. I drew it forth instantly and examined it critically. It was indeed a rare and beautiful blade, such as would have delighted the eye of a practised swordsman. I balanced the trustworthy weapon easily in my hand. It fitted my arm as if it had grown to my palm.

" 'Tis a rare and beautiful weapon, if I am a judge."

"I think, from the way you handle it, that you are."

I shot it back into its sheath, clasped the belt about my waist, and instantly felt a thousand times more manly than before. The steel dangling against my legs seemed to add the finishing touch of completeness to my disguise. I was now a man indeed.

"Here," said the advocate, extending his hand with a purse, "is the money."

I sought to thrust it, womanlike, into the bosom of my shirt beneath the ruffles.

Master Dunner laughed.

"You have a pocket, sir, where such things are kept by men."

Once more I blushed.

"Your reminder is a good one," said I in some confusion, searching in the breast of my coat until I found the receptacle. "I may appear manly enough, but I lack practice in the niceties of the masquerade."

"That will come in time, madam," said the old man.

"Ah, yes," was my smiling answer, "but, as you noted before, time is what we lack. Yet I must e'en do my best with what I have. Where is the horse, and the mails?"

He pointed toward the door.

"In the alley at the back of the house. The mails are strapped to the saddle. They contain a change of linen and various other articles. I saw to their bestowing."

" Men's clothing or women's? "

" Men's, of course. From Lord Carthew's wardrobe. What should a young gallant like you be doing with women's gear? "

" True," said I. " You are right. May not the horse be brought around to the front of the house? "

" I think it safer and more secluded in the alley. Suspicion is easily excited in Edinburgh now, and to see so splendid a cavalier as yourself issuing from so mean an abode as this might give rise to curious question. This is our only haven. I would hold it inviolate for your return until tomorrow night."

" You are right, Master Dunner," said I. " And now I must go. I can think of nothing more. What's o'clock? "

" 'Twas on the stroke of nine as I entered the house."

" If I ride carefully, I should be at Cockenzie before five. That will give me ample time. If our calculations fail not, I will meet Sir Hugh there."

I paused.

" And may God aid you and defend the right! " said the old man solemnly.

" Amen," said I. " And now good-bye."

I extended my hand once more. Mine ancient friend bowed over it, but I prevented him. I stepped toward him. Indeed, I overtowered him quite on account of his diminutive stature and his lameness, so that I bent my head and kissed him on the forehead without ceremony or hesitation.

" Good-bye, true friend," I said.

He was mightily touched by this mark of condescension. His thin face flushed.

" I would to God," he cried, " that I were young and strong and whole that I might ride for you or with you. 'Tis I who play the woman's part."

" Nay," said I, touched in turn by his generous words. " Without you this could not be. Will you have access to my father?"

" Yes, by the favour of the Lord Chief Justice, who is well affected toward me. What shall I tell him?"

" Tell him everything. Tell him, on the faith of the last Clanranald, I will have the warrant, or . . ."

I paused.

" Or what, your ladyship?"

"Or I will await him on the other side," I answered, looking away.

"God forbid!" earnestly protested the old man, sinking down and burying his head in his hands by the table.

"Look for me with the warrant to-morrow night," said I, forcing a smile lest I should break down, with my hand on the door.

"Wait!" he cried. "Don't think of bringing me the warrant. Destroy it instantly, tear it up when you get your hands upon it, or, better still, burn it. Here!"

He drew from his pocket a flint and steel in a little case. He was one of the few who practised the new-fangled habit of smoking the Virginia weed. I never could see what pleasure he got from it.

"Take these. You can kindle fire with them. Burn the warrant, should you be fortunate enough to lay hands upon it. Scraps may be pieced; ashes tell no tales. You understand the use of these things?"

I had often seen him light his pipe.

"Entirely," said I. "You shall see me, then, to-morrow night, with the statement that the warrant is destroyed."

"I pray so, I pray so!" cried the old man as I passed out of the room.

Now, I had—I suppose I should say it to my shame—often ridden astride at home. While I ordinarily rode as was the habit of my sex, sometimes, in wild mountain excursions through the forest glens or on hunting trips and adventurous journeys in the Highlands with my father and some faithful servitors, I had perforce and of necessity been compelled to ride astride. Therefore, it was no novelty for me to have between my legs a good horse.

Advocate learned in the law though he might be, Master Dunner was a rare judge of horse-flesh, I thought, or else he had wit enough to employ unquestioned talent for that purpose, for I never saw a sweeter, better-bred steed than that led by a horse-boy in the alley. He was perhaps a trifle undersized for a full-grown man's charger, but for my weight and build he was admirable: a deep French bay in exquisite condition. The saddle and mails behind were new, and the horse was equipped *point device.*

You see from this that I had studied French. Indeed, I was much better educated than the majority of my sex, to whom all learning save the

simplest was a sealed book. My father had taken
interest in me to teach me things, and I even knew
where that quotation from Master Shakespeare
came which my advocate had used, for my Lord
and I had read the plays together and liked them
well.

Slipping a coin into the horse-boy's hand, I
stepped by the side of my horse, patted him a few
moments, fondled him to make his acquaintance,
wished that I had brought a bit of sugar for him,
but made up for that default by my tender usage
of him. Then I sprang lightly to the saddle and
cantered slowly down the alley.

I was entirely familiar with Edinburgh and I
easily avoided the main highways, taking alleys
and by-streets, until I came to the gate in the city
wall which gave out to the east, or Dunbar Road.
Doubtless I made a fine sight with my handsome
clothes, my easy bearing, my youthful face and my
gallant steed. The soldiers at the gate, thinking
they had to do with a wealthy gentleman, saluted
as I passed, and I took some comfort in acknowl-
edging, with a careless wave of my gauntleted
hand, their respective duties.

By rights I should have been accompanied by a
servant on another horse, but I did not stay long

enough to let any question me for that lack, for
so soon as I was clear of the town, and a turn of
the road hid me from possible observation and
scrutiny by the soldiers, I put spurs to my horse.
Indeed a word would have been sufficient, but the
spurs were upon my boots and I touched him with
one. His bound nearly unseated me, by the way.

I was minded to distance possible pursuit by
putting a long space between me and the town
as soon as possible. There were two roads before me that led westerly; one crookedly along
the shore, and the other inland a mile or so. The
shore road was the more frequented, the broader
and better highway; it was also somewhat longer,
since it followed the windings of the coast, while
that inland, through wooded and farming country and over the hills, was straighter, shorter, and
more direct. It was also much less travelled, and
therefore I was less apt to meet with question
and more apt to avoid pursuit, should any be
made. Accordingly, I chose the inland way. The
two roads met at a place called Musselburgh, and
from thence the way ran directly along the shore
to the tavern where I confidently expected to meet
my friend.

I was an astonishingly good horseman—how

I dropped into the masculine in talking of myself, I thought!—and I knew that, if I pushed my horse too hard at the first, he would be spent for the rest of the day. Therefore, after going perhaps five or six miles at a rapid pace, I checked him, and thereafter proceeded in a more reasonable way.

I met no one of any importance, save yokels driving hay-wains and wagons of produce to the city, travelling pedlars, a little company of merchants, a stray soldier, to all of whom I gave good-day and passed on, none offering to molest me. My heart, which had beat high at the sight of the first-comer with all sorts of vague anticipation of disaster, at last became quite indifferent to any approaching traveller, and I flattered myself that I need be under no apprehension whatever of any one penetrating my disguise or seeking to harm me.

Nevertheless, I was careful to see that my pistols were loose in the holsters; that the priming made them fit for instant discharge, and that my sword-hilt was pulled a little forward ready to hand, should anybody attempt to stop me. I was determined to show my mettle and not to yield until the last extremity. There were, of course, high-

waymen abroad, but they rarely molested people
in open daylight. By nightfall, please God, I
would be safely sheltered in The Black Douglas
at Cockenzie.

It was noon when I cantered gallantly down the
streets of Musselburgh. I had determined to rest
there an hour to bait my horse, to get my dinner,
and to consider further what my plans and future
work should be. I drew up before the door of a
comfortable-looking hostelry. Stable-boys came
running; the landlord himself appeared in the
doorway of his inn. I descended, called for a
meal which I demanded should be of roast beef
and other substantials accompanied by a bottle of
wine, thus doing violence to my natural dainty
appetite, which would have preferred a fowl and
cold water. I also engaged a private parlour and
was accordingly served in private. I spent an hour
thus very quietly and pleasantly without dis-
turbance.

Now, I had been brought up very unconven-
tionally in a way that would have scandalised my
female relatives, had I enjoyed any, and which
doubtless did scandalise certain neighbouring
dames whose seats adjoined our own, but, nevertheless, I was a woman and I had never been

absolutely free, independent, and unrestrained before.

I confess to a delightful sensation of excitement at my present situation. I think I must have had all the daring and adventurous spirit of the famous Clanranalds, and to be thus mounted on a good horse with money in my purse, a good sword by my side, a great adventure before me, filled me with joy. I had all the confidence of youth and inexperience, and all the hopefulness of woman, that somehow I should be able to bring about my desire, and that my romantic action in attempting this wild masquerade would result in the saving of the life of my noble father.

I thought with considerable complacency that this exploit of mine would entitle me to something more than a mention of my name in the family chronicles, and that perhaps I might be counted as worthy the best traditions of our ancient house. In anticipation, I could feel my Lord clasp me in his arms when I had saved his life and bless me for my daring, although I well knew that he would have died rather than give his consent to such an amazing undertaking.

The good meal, the wine, of which I drank

but sparingly, pouring the rest out of the window when no one was looking, refreshed me greatly. With a new zeal, therefore, I mounted my horse, flung the landlord a guinea, at which he bowed himself nearly to the floor, and cantered down the street through the town and out upon the broad ocean highway.

The sea breeze, with all its splendid freshness, lifted the close curls of my full wig, fanned my brow, and cooled my cheeks in the most exhilarating way. I rode rapidly enough, observing my horse possessed of all the qualities of speed and stamina that his appearance had indicated, and, without anything untoward or exciting happening, about five o'clock in the evening I drew up at the Black Douglas Inn, at Cockenzie.

Cockenzie was merely a huddle of little houses, with nothing on earth to recommend it except the old inn pleasantly placed on a bluff headland overlooking the sea. It was the only house of any pretence whatever in the little fishing village, and before it I drew rein. Judicious inquiries elicited the fact that at the moment I was the only guest of the inn. I bespake the best chamber, ordered myself substantial supper, saw personally to the quartering and care of my horse, washed my own face and hands, went out of the rear door of the inn, walked to the edge of the high bluff, and sat down on a rude bench overlooking the sea, while waiting for my supper, and pondered carefully on my next step.

I had address enough to find out from the inn-maid who saw me to my apartment that no such traveller as I suspected Sir Hugh Richmond to be had passed by within that day or the day before. Therefore, I was in time. I had no doubt that this very night he would appear on the scene. Master Dunner's information was such as to carry assurance to him, and I depended upon its accuracy. Sitting and watching the ocean, I tried to decide upon my best course when I should at last be confronted by mine enemy.

Chapter
III

How I ate, drank, and gamed with Sir Hugh Richmond, under whom I would fain see Service

FOR all my cogitations, I had settled upon nothing, and I was not only surprised but confused when there stepped out on the porch and made toward me—the clatter of his boots upon the pavement caused me to turn my head—a cavalier, whom I instantly divined to be the bearer of our evil tidings. Abstractly, I had a welcome in my heart for him such as Pharaoh of old entertained for similar messengers, and I purposed to meet him in much the same way, too; concretely, my first thought was one of pleased surprise at his appearance.

He was tall, well-knit, well-bronzed, of darker skin and eyes than mine. His face was handsome in a stern and somewhat martial way. His bearing was that of a soldier and accorded well with the rich uniform he wore. I observed that he made directly to me, and, therefore, I inferred that he had come to seek me. I was annoyed at myself that I had enjoyed no more time for preparation for the meeting. I must have been deeply absorbed in my thoughts, I decided, not to have heard the clatter he made riding up to the door of the inn on the other side.

I had taken off my hat—heavy, clumsy felt thing that it was!—but, as the new-comer approached, I clapped it firmly on my head and rose, resisting with difficulty a wild inclination to wrap my riding-coat about my legs like the skirt of a dress.

My officer stopped a few paces from me, clapped his heels together, removed his hat with a sharp military gesture, and bowed quite gracefully before me.

" Sir," said he in a firm, authoritative voice, due perhaps to his habit of command, " may I introduce myself? I am Sir Hugh Richmond, captain in the King's Guards."

" My name is . . ." replied I, bowing in my turn, " is . . ."

What was my name? In my hurry it had not occurred to me to fix upon any. I paused stupidly enough while the gallant captain fixed his dark eyes upon me in surprised inquiry. I blurted out the first that came into my mind.

" Henry Carthew," I said.

" I am glad to have the honour of your acquaintance, Mr. Carthew," continued the soldier agreeably.

As he spoke, he smiled slightly. His face changed at once, and I thought, when he smiled, I had never seen a pleasanter-looking man. It was as if the real man had given a glimpse of himself behind the cloud with which habit and military discipline had shrouded him. Oh, but he was good to look on then!

" The pleasure, sir, is mine. I am honoured in the acquaintance of so distinguished a soldier as Sir Hugh Richmond."

Another look of surprise came to the face of the officer.

" You have heard of me, sir? " he asked, not without a certain pride.

" Your charge at Sedgemoor hath been told of even in Scotland."

" 'Twas naught," he said carelessly. " I take it, sir, that you are not a soldier? "

" Only by inclination," replied I bravely. " I am contemplating service, however, and indeed, sir, 'twas for that I came hither in the hope of meeting you."

" Of meeting me? "

" Even so," I answered boldly, feeling that by happy chance I had stumbled upon an excellent excuse for my presence and interest. " We have heard in Edinburgh that you were on your way hither with warrants for the execution of the Earl of Clanranald and other rebels against His Majesty."

" Faith, sir," was the reply, " my name, my history, and business seem well enough known in these parts. And how, may I ask, was this news bruited abroad? "

" Express riders from the south have stated that you were charged with the delivery of the King's warrants for those high enough for His Majesty to take personal interest in," I answered promptly.

" 'Fore God, sir," exclaimed Sir Hugh, laughing lightly, " with that rumour running ahead of me, I wonder some one did not endeavour to despoil me of my warrants in the interest of the condemned! "

" Sir," said I, " we are all loyal men in these parts."

I smiled as I spoke.

"Since Sedgemoor," returned the captain, sharing in my amusement.

"Ay, since Sedgemoor, and I believe there is no man in Scotland would molest you."

"But the adherents of Clanranald? I mention him since he is of the greater rank," he asked curiously.

I shrugged my shoulders. 'Twas excellent well done i' faith. I doubt if Mistress Nell Gwynn herself could have acted better. Although my heart was beating like to choke me, I gave no outward sign.

"He hath made his bed," I said, with what affectation of indifference I could muster, "let him lie upon it."

"'Tis like to be a long sleep then," returned my captain grimly, "for the warrant spells his death."

"So we have heard," said I.

I had to bite my lip and turn away for the moment, but I put such iron constraint upon myself as enabled me to awaken no suspicion in the captain's mind.

"Poor gentleman!" he said, after a little pause. "I never had errand that I liked less to discharge. But this work does not interest you, young sir."

Oh, did it not? I never was so interested in all my life.

" Nor did I break upon your solitude to discuss the King's business or my own. I learned from the landlord that a guest had preceded me, and that a gentleman had ordered supper who sat in loneliness out here, whence I made bold to interrupt your reverie and propose that we should share the table. I have had so little society since entering Scotland that I pine for a little free intercourse with my equals. Most gentlemen have avoided me, due perhaps to the rumour of which you speak."

" You are very welcome to such poor companionship as I can give you," said I. " And indeed, as I told you, I had come here to seek you with view to entering the King's service. I'm a gentleman of some small fortune. They call me the Laird of Lochnaven."

" Your age, young sir?" said the captain, surveying me thoughtfully.

" My age!" I exclaimed, with a woman's natural reluctance to declare it. " Is it necessary that I . . ."

The captain threw back his head and laughed boisterously.

" You are as timorous about giving it as if you were a girl."

" Twenty! " exclaimed I in my deepest voice and most imperious manner. "And, sir, I would thank you to modify your allusion to any timidity you may falsely suspect me of."

I laid my hand on my sword and was glad to feel the touch of the hilt. It gave me something to still my agitation.

" Thou art a good lad," said the captain genially, clapping me heavily upon the shoulder, " if but a slight one. I like your pluck, Master Carthew, and I have no doubt we will turn you into a brave soldier yet."

" I have, I trust, interest enough to procure me a cornetcy."

" Interest is well enough, but, hark ye, a word in your ear. What you Scots call siller is about the most interesting appeal any one can make to King James."

" I will e'en have a supply of that."

" Well, then," returned the captain, " the matter can be easily arranged, I make no doubt. We shall take further counsel on 't to-morrow. If agreeable to you, I should like to have you in my own company of guards. There's a vacancy or two since Sedgemoor, and I'll own my heart warms to you, lad."

"Nothing would please me better," said I, delighted at the success of my ruse, "than the prospect of service under so distinguished a master of the art as yourself."

"You talk like a book, boy," said the captain, not ill-pleased, however, at the compliment. "I foresee we shall get along vastly well. I had been pining for the sight of a woman in all these lonely rides, but you will take the place of one as well as any man on earth could."

Could he suspect me?

"Sir, sir!" I cried, "do I infer that you think me womanish?"

"What a tinder-box it is!" laughed the captain. "I only meant your wit and your spirit would go far to render other company unnecessary. Come," he resumed, "loose your hold upon your sword. I am too old to fight with you, and in too peaceful a mood for quarrel to-night, especially about nothing."

"Gentlemen," said the landlord, coming out of the door and approaching us, "your supper is served. Not hearing to the contrary and seeing you together, sirs, I have ventured to set it at one table."

" You have done well," I replied.

" Excellent i' faith," commented my companion genially.

And together we turned toward the house. It was, indeed, a noble supper that was set before us. My fellow-traveller insisted that, as I was the first-comer and had done the ordering, to me appertained the head of the table. He proved a good trencherman likewise, and made much mock of my small appetite, alleging that all good soldiers were of necessity good feeders. I did my best to follow his generous example, but I am afraid I minced more as a woman than ate vigorously as a man.

It had been dusk outside when Sir Hugh had approached me. The dim light of the candles in the big parlour in which we supped was not more favourable to a disclosure of my secret than the twilight outside. I felt confident that no suspicions had been awakened in the soldier's mind, although how I could have borne his keen scrutiny in the full blaze of day was a doubtful question. I did not mean to bear it, so far as I was con-

cerned, under those conditions if it could in any
wise be helped.

"If I be not indiscreet, Sir Hugh," said I,
during a pause in the meal, "I take it that you are
an unmarried man?"

"You take it right, Master Carthew. A soldier loves all ladies; he marries none."

"A poor lookout for womankind if the best
men are in the army," said I, bridling.

"'Tis the stern necessity of the trade," he returned coolly. "Wedlock and the sword go not
well together. Have you a sweetheart, young
sir?" he asked in his turn.

"I?" I exclaimed indignantly. "Certainly
not. No. Yes. . . . That is . . ."

"Keep thy secret, lad. Do you come soldiering
with me, you will have one in every town where
you are stationed longer than a fortnight."

"Are soldiers, then, so fickle?"

"They are truth itself," he paused, "to the
nearest fair," he added.

He lifted his glass and surveyed it a moment
with half-shut eyes.

"I give you a toast. To the nearest fair!"

He drank his. I sipped mine. He noticed my
abstemiousness.

"When you love harder, you drink deeper and fight better," he said sagely.

"Doubtless," said I. "And yet," I ran on, "the romances tell us of the constant devotion of the knight to his lady. Of how the soldier adventures far and wide and yet remains true to his one ideal at home."

"Such hath not been my experience. War and soldiering you will find are not as they are writ of in books."

"You have questioned me; I have no doubt that you will permit me to question you," I said in my turn.

"You are not under my command yet," said the captain, smiling at my presumption. "Ask what you will."

"Then there is no especial lady to whom your thoughts revert?"

"None, or rather there are a dozen," was the prompt reply.

I do not know why I should have felt glad at this, or what particular interest I had in Sir Hugh Richmond's love affairs, but he had rather flouted the idea of my sex, and, although I wore the trews for the time being, I could not forget that I was yet a woman. I should have liked to

teach this red-coated Sassenach a thing or two,
and I really longed for an opportunity to show
him that we girls of Scotland were not to be so
lightly dismissed as all that.

" You see, lad, I have campaigned in many
countries, and have seen many women. God bless
them all! I have liked an eye here, a cheek there,
a foot and ankle yonder, a fine figure in this place,
a merry laugh in another, spirit in a third, meek-
ness in a fourth, but I have never seen one, that
had all these traits and characteristics blended, that
measured up to my own ideal."

" And what is your ideal, may I ask? You will
forgive my curiosity. I am less a man than I
seem." It was verging on the truth with a vengeance. " I have lived sequestered most of my life,
and you cannot think how it interests me to have
the views of so experienced a man of the world
and so veteran a soldier as yourself upon this
subject."

He looked sharply at me as I sat at the head
of the table toying with my glass, as if he suspected some hidden meaning in my words, but I
never appeared more innocent and guileless in my
life than at that moment.

"Well," said he, " 'tis a strange turn the conversation hath taken, but I know not why I should not humour you. My ideal maid, then, will be a woman who is first of all tall, about your own size. She shall have hair of sunshine colour and eyes of blue, and her cheek shall be fair to contrast with my own dark visage. In shape she shall be plump, not slender. Her hands shapely and white, but strong. I want none of your puling, lackadaisical, sentimental misses. She shall be a woman of spirit, one with courage enough not to run a-squeak at the sight of a mouse, one that can handle a sword or press the trigger of a weapon and discharge it without shutting her eyes at the report, one who can ride by my side if need be. As for learning, I want none of your dull and stupid minxes. Let her be read so that she can talk about something beside fallals, furbelows, children, and housewifery; one who could meet me on some terms of equality, who can preside gracefully over my establishment and mother my many children."

I thanked God that the candle-light did not disclose the furious colour in my cheek.

" Think you," said I, " that such a woman would be a good mother? "

" She would bring forth a race of soldiers," was

the answer, " which is what I should like best to father."

" And what have you," I asked, forgetting that I was not a man in my indignation at his unbounded and condescending assurance, " to offer in exchange for this female paragon you have described ? "

"What have I to offer? " He started to his feet violently and leaned over the table. " This is past endurance, sir," he said in sudden temper, striking the board hotly with his fist. " What do you mean? "

" Nothing, nothing offensive," I returned quickly, endeavouring to keep my temper and be calm as his anger rose. " 'Tis but a jest. I meant no offence."

His temper subsided as suddenly as it had arisen.

" As you say," he answered, after a moment's reflection; " 'tis idle talk. You ask what I have to offer? Truth to tell, I never thought of it in that way."

" But would it not be fair," I asked, " to take stock of the qualities to be exchanged for those you have demanded? "

" Fair, yes; but a man hardly likes to appraise

himself; in fact, I doubt that he can do it truthfully. Yet I'll try. I am thirty-two, heart-whole and fancy-free, the possessor of a rentroll of five or six thousand a year, hold a commission in the King's Guards, am sound in wind and limb, good in temper, possess some small learning which I got at Oxford, and—faith, that's all."

I laughed. I could not help it.

" That's the assurance of mankind," I said at last. " Do you give me leave to speak frankly about you? "

" I invite you to do so," returned the captain complacently.

" Here you are, just an ordinary, commonplace soldier approaching middle life, of good birth and reasonable fortune, declaring that nothing can suit you but the never-to-be-realised ideal you have described."

" You are, indeed, frank," returned Sir Hugh resentfully.

" I am," I answered, " and I will be more so. If you wish, I will give you my own ideal of womankind."

" I should like to hear what your vast experience has evolved," returned the other, somewhat sarcastically.

" She shall be small, tender, meek, adoring, dark of hair and eye, dainty and nice of taste and appearance. She shall hang upon my words, attempt no equality with me, come to my hand, and . . ."

" You want a dog, not a woman," said the captain, laughing. "When you have seen more, your views will differ."

" It may be."

" And what, pray, is your ideal man? " he asked lightly.

" He shall be tall and strong and brave and true, with bright hair and blue eyes, a soldier by profession, and fierce to all the world but reserving his tender side for me. . . . I mean for the woman that he loves," I added hastily to cover my slip. " He shall worship her and think her as far above him as the stars."

" You ought to marry your ideal man to your ideal woman," interposed the captain jocosely, " and see what the result would be. 'Fore God, sir, I'd like to observe such a union. Meanwhile, give me leave as an older man. We have talked enough sentiment for a boxful of French romances. It hath made me thirsty. Another bottle of wine, pray." He rapped on the table as he spoke, and bade it brought. "And then, when the remains of our supper shall be cleared away, I propose that we pass an hour in play before we retire for the night. I at least must make an early start to-morrow."

"I am agreeable," said I. "We have exchanged views upon our ladies and their cavaliers, and I am willing to back my luck against your own."

"With what shall we play?"

"With dice," I answered. "At any game of skill with such a veteran as you I would be at too great a disadvantage."

"True," said the captain, looking me over carefully. "Thou art a queer lad, but I like thee."

"The regard is mutual," said I. "What shall the stakes be?"

"Let us play for shillings," he said after a thoughtful moment.

His intent was so obvious that I could not bear the imputation.

"Nay, for guineas!" I cried.

"Done," said the captain. "Here's rare sporting blood, I see."

When we parted for the night an hour later,

Captain Richmond was near a hundred pounds richer than when he sat down. It was purely a game of chance, this throwing of the dice, and yet, I know not how it was, luck was steadily against me. I had sense enough to reserve a few guineas for my roadway needs, but with the rest I had played desperately till all were gone.

It was the first time that I had ever tempted fortune with the ivory. My father had never allowed me so to do. The fascination of it was great, but hardly enough to compensate for the repentance I felt for even this modest depletion of the totally inadequate store that Master Dunner would be able to gather for our great purpose.

Too late. I was horror-struck at my folly and my imprudence. Something of my feelings must have appeared in my face, for, on a sudden, Captain Richmond pushed the heap of guineas across the table toward me.

" There, lad," he said most courteously, " I did but jest with you. Take thy guineas back. We have had a pleasant evening together, and I shall be happier if your gold is in your own purse rather than in mine."

But this I could not brook.

" Sir," said I, " I may appear a poor loser, but

'tis in appearance only. You have fairly won the stakes and they are yours. Nay," I cried as I saw him about to speak again, " to protest further would be to insult me! "

" As you will," said the captain coolly, " and, if I may say so, I congratulate you upon being a good loser. You shall have your revenge another time, with Fortune, I trust, in a more complacent mood. Which way do you ride tomorrow? "

" To Edinburgh," I answered.

" Do you make an early start? "

" At daybreak," I replied.

" We shall ride together then and discourse further."

" Upon our ladies? " I asked impudently to cover my dismay.

" Nay, upon your commission in my company," he answered.

" With all my heart," said I.

"Here's to our further acquaintance," he continued, pouring himself another glass of wine. " And so, good-night."

Chapter
IV

Wherein I played the Highwayman and what befell me on the Road

I RETIRED to my chamber in a great state of perturbation. I had made the captain's acquaintance; I had some idea of his temperament and quality; I had gained, to a certain degree his confidence and won, in some measure, his regard, it appeared. There was no doubt about his liking for me. Yet I was no nearer the accomplishment of my purpose than before, and the sight of the captain had not reassured me as to its entire practicability. He could jest and discourse idly with me, and play and eat and drink like any other man and soldier, but I instinctively realised that in an emergency it would be a bold, a ready, and a resourceful person who could get the better of such as he.

In the parlour of the inn he was one man; on the road to-morrow he would be another. I could match him at repartee easily enough, but when it came to a quick eye, a steady hand, a daring heart,

I would be sadly lacking. There was no comparison between us on the score of efficiency. In so much as I fancied that I surpassed other women in physical ability, so I was sure that in the same degree he surpassed other men. Only the desperation lent to me by my father's grave peril would tend to equalise conditions between us.

I said that he liked me. I liked him. He differed from the gentlemen with whom I had been acquainted. He was more a man of the world than any. His coolness, his personal distinction, even his age, attracted me. I wished that he had been on my side. I could have trusted him with the wild undertaking I was now endeavouring to bring about, and I could have rested quite confident that he would succeed in it.

Yes, marvellous as it may seem, I could have viewed his claiming the inevitable reward with a certain degree of equanimity, if equanimity be the word to describe a wildly fluttering, beating heart such as my own. He inspired my confidence and something more.

My mind swiftly reverted to his ideal woman. I was not vain and foolish, I trust, and yet was I not tall and fair? Was there not sunshine, or had there not been sunshine in my long locks before I cut them off? Were my eyes not the blue of which he spoke? Was not my figure plump? I examined what was visible of it with another burning blush, wondering if he had marked it. Could I not ride and hold a sword and fire a weapon without shutting my eyes? Did I not have learning enough to match me with this . . .

Pshaw, the man was nothing, could be nothing, to me except my enemy. And all such speculations were indeed idle. If I had time and could appear before him in my proper person, I might win his devotion did I desire it, I made no doubt.

But I had no time. I had to get from him to-morrow, in some way, by some means, the fatal warrant. How? His chamber was across the hall from mine. Could I effect entrance therein in the middle of the night, and, unobserved, steal the despatch-case in which, doubtless, he would carry it? It might be done, but suppose he awoke and seized me there and found me a woman?

I shivered at the thought. What would he think of me in such a case? On the other hand, what did I care what he thought of me so long as I got the warrant?

But if I were caught, would I not have to pay

the price, lose all, and get nothing? It could not be.

Was there any way in which I could win it from him by finesse? None. By cajolery? Men do not cajole men. And if I said, or he discovered, that I was a woman, I would be helpless.

There was but one way: I should have to take it from him by force. I, a woman, to all intents a slender stripling, would have to overmaster this veteran soldier! Well, I swore that I would do it. I would stop him in the highway, be the risk what it might.

A long time I made plans, only to dismiss one after another until, at last, I hit upon something that seemed to give at least faint promise of success. I would stake all upon that. I could do nothing else.

Slipping off my boots and coat and loosening my clothes slightly, I threw myself down upon the bed, having left directions that I should be called by four of the clock, and fell into a troubled sleep, full of anxious dreams born of my strange plight.

I was up betimes, hastily dressed myself, and descended to the taproom. It was still dark. I knew that Sir Hugh would not be called until daybreak, that he would order breakfast ere he started, and that I should have probably an hour for my purposes. Bidding the sleepy maid to get me some kind of a meal, I went out to the stables to look to my horse.

There were only two strange horses in the stalls, mine and this soldier's. Our saddles hung side by side on pegs. Awakening the ill-tempered hostler, I despatched him to the taproom to bring my saddle-bags and to draw a bucket of water for my horse. The instant he left the stable, I ran to Sir Hugh's saddle and drew the pistols from the holsters. They were a pair of heavy, serviceable, soldier-like weapons. I had a fit of trembling at the idea that they might be pointed at me.

To unscrew the ramrods and draw the charges was the work of a few moments. I was in a desperate hurry and, fortunately, got the pistols, still primed, back in the holsters before the stable-boy came in. I tossed him a crown to relieve his spleen, and bade him get my horse ready quietly and bring him to the door of the inn within ten minutes.

Then I went back, hastily partook of such breakfast as was set before me and paid my reckoning to the landlord, who had by this time come sleepily down the stairs. I left a message for Sir Hugh Richmond that, being nervous and having passed a sleepless night, I had risen early, breakfasted and had ridden on ahead, and would progress slowly that he might overtake me on the road at his convenience. Then I clambered to the saddle and rode away in a rare state of perturbation indeed.

Coming to Cockenzie the day before, I had marked a place where the road bent sharply away from the shore, on account of the broken nature of the cliffs, and plunged for the space of a mile through a stretch of woodland. Such a place, if fortune gave me the least favour, would be most advantageous for my purposes. There I had determined to play the part of highwayman.

When I reached the spot, I drew away from the road beneath the trees and made a careful survey of the situation. I found that I could sit my horse under the shelter of the trees, myself unseen, although with a clear glimpse of the open road leading to the forest, and could easily burst out upon a traveller coming around the bend without giving him the least previous warning.

It was still early in the morning—in fact, it was not yet full dawn—when I reached this point, some miles from the inn, and I hoped that no other traveller on the road would inconveniently appear to balk me in my desire. Fortunately no one was abroad then. The place and road were lonely and deserted.

I had plenty of time to make all my preparations. I carefully examined my pistols and saw that my sword was ready at hand. If Sir Hugh had examined his own weapons critically and had recharged them, if I did not kill him first I should probably be shot dead.

The alternatives before me were simple, I reflected with a faint heart. Before an hour, I should possibly be murdered or be a murderess myself. I liked neither the one possibility nor the other. If Sir Hugh had not recharged his pistols, it was likely that I could get his despatch-bag, but probably only after I had shot him, for I realised that a man such as he would never give up a charge upon a mere demand or threat such as I had at first hoped might suffice.

Well, I knew all this before. There was no use repining at it now. I played for a great stake— my father's life. That stood higher with me than the life of any other man or woman, including my own. I would carry out the enterprise with determination to the end as I had planned, whatever the consequences to myself. But I would that the necessity had never been laid upon me, a helpless maiden.

It is simple enough and easy enough to say all this, but it was by no means easy or pleasant to think on at the time, and I own that no hour I ever spent dragged as that one. Indeed, if the undertaking had been put off another hour, I believe I could scarce have mustered courage enough to carry the affair through even for my dear Lord's life.

It seemed such a pity that no other way presented itself. Certainly, I did not want to shoot this unsuspecting officer. I had almost rather he shot me. Instantly my imagination ran away with me, and I pictured him lying lifeless and bloody at my feet, or myself in like case. And in these speculations I own I quite lost sight of the headsman's axe and the block awaiting my father in Edinburgh with only me to stay them.

I was becoming quite unmanned when I caught the sound of a horse's footfalls on the road. I rose to my feet from the grassy bank where I had been resting, ran back under the trees, mounted my own horse, rode to the bend of the road, and

stationed myself out of sight behind a thick
growth of underbrush. I peered cautiously down
the road before I took this position and discovered that the oncoming horseman was the red-
coated Sir Hugh.

The sun had just risen, and the open road was
full of light, although the place where I stood
was still in quite deep shadow. My nervousness,
I am thankful to say, largely left me in the moment of emergency, and I observed with satisfaction that the hand which held the pistol resting
lightly across the pommel of the saddle was quite
steady.

Sir Hugh was pushing his horse at a smart pace.
Fortunately for me, however, he reined in just as
he approached the wood and scanned it curiously,
like the careful soldier that he was. There was
nothing suspicious, however, and he rode on rather
carelessly. As he came around the bend, I was instantly disclosed. I endeavoured to sit and to look
as negligently as was possible. I don't think anything in my appearance awakened his suspicion,
for he checked his horse, and turned slowly toward
me with an air in which were mingled surprise and
satisfaction.

"Good-morrow, Master Carthew!" he cried,

with a wave of his hand and quite buoyantly. " I
thought I had lost you. What strange freak
made you get up and ride ahead? "

The moment had arrived. It was now or
never. If I waited, I could not do it. He looked
so handsome in the full light. He bore himself so
bravely and seemed so glad to chance upon me
again. Quick as a flash, I lifted my right arm and
pointed the pistol fair at his heart, although I
prayed that I might not have to press the trigger.

" Stop where you are! " I cried peremptorily.
" If you move a hand, I'll put a bullet through
your heart, sir."

I never saw such blank astonishment in any human face. At other times I might have laughed
at it.

" Why, good God! " he exclaimed when he
could master his amazement a little.

"Silence! " I cried. And my voice, I am sorry
to say, lost the deep pitch to which I had striven
to subdue it and rang highly feminine. " I mean
what I say," I continued. " If you do not obey
my commands, I shall be under the painful necessity of killing you."

Instinctively confronted by such a weapon,—
and my hand, I thrilled to see, did not even yet

tremble, though my heart beat so it was like to choke me,—he had remained absolutely motionless.

" Is this a jest, young sir? " he at last inquired, frowning.

" No jest as you will see, but I have no time for talk. I want . . ."

" Your hundred guineas, I suppose," he sneered. " Why, I offered you them last night. You could have taken them like a gentleman instead of filching them like a thief."

" I want no guineas! " I protested.

But he was too quick for me. With a movement of lightning-like rapidity, the which I had not imagined him or any man capable of, he bent forward, whipped a pistol out of his holster, pointed it at me, and pulled the trigger. For one brief second my eyes did close. There was a flash in the pan—thank God, nothing more. I had not, in spite of my fright, lowered my weapon.

" Curses on the pistol! " he cried.

I laughed.

" If you do not instantly drop it in the road, I will pull the trigger."

I think he realised now that I was in earnest,

for he unclosed his fingers and the pistol fell to the ground.

" Now," said I, " you need not look at the other weapon, for I myself drew the charges this morning."

I was sure of my man now and I could afford to temporise.

" You can examine it yourself," I continued confidently, " to make sure that further resistance on your part is futile. Only I warn you that, if you turn it never so little toward me, I will let you have this pistol, and I assure you it is thoroughly charged."

With this permission he at once drew the other pistol from the holster, examined it, and, by command, dropped it in the road beside its useless fellow.

" You have me at a disadvantage, Master Carthew. I am soldier enough to know when I am beaten. What do you wish of me? " he asked me quietly enough; too quietly, had I but known it.

" Your despatches," I said.

" My despatches? "

" You can understand the English language," I continued, " even when spoken by a Scot. Hand them over, or I swear to you . . ."

" This is foolish preparation for a commission in the King's service, boy."

" I desire no service with that false King," I answered recklessly.

" Are you for Monmouth, then ? "

" I am."

" Why, Lord love ye, boy, the Duke hath been executed long since on Tower Hill, and . . ."

" I'm for myself, then ! " I cried. " We waste words. Your despatches ! "

" I have liked you," said the man gently, looking at me quite pleasantly, with a little smile upon his lips. " There is the making in you of a rare soldier, for all your slender, almost feminine appearance."

At that my pistol did waver for a second,—it was terribly heavy, I found, extended out before me,—but only for a second.

" Be advised. This is high treason. You will die for it surely."

" On my own head be the consequences. I appreciate the kindness of your warning. Once and for all, will you give over the packet."

" Needs must with such a persuader," he said, smiling.

He reached his left hand into his breast pocket

and drew forth a heavy leather wallet. He extended his hand toward me. I was new at the business; I should have had him drop it in the road and ride on, but such was my eagerness for it that I spoke to my horse and advanced a pace to meet him.

I nearly had cause to rue forever that miscalculation, for while still extending the packet with one hand, with the other he reached down with astonishing quickness, drew my other pistol from the holster, and pulled the trigger. Our horses were both in motion at the time. My only salvation was to fire upon him, and, even as the weapon which he had seized spoke, so did mine. I felt a sharp, agonising pain in my left shoulder. I knew that I had been hit; how seriously I could not tell, nor could I give much thought to my condition, for my interest was in him.

Fortune had favoured me, for as I stared, my left arm dangling, Sir Hugh threw up his hands, his face went white; I could see a red smudge on his forehead. He reeled in his saddle, fell back, slipped sideways, and slid down to the road. Both horses were in a great state of excitement. Sir Hugh's foot was still in the stirrup. I had managed to control mine by a word; his own horse

started off. Sir Hugh would have been dragged
and battered to pieces in a few bounds. I barred
the way and, with my right hand, I caught his
horse's bridle and brought the well-trained animal
instantly to a stop. I found that, although my
coat-sleeve was stained with blood, I could still
move my arm, which rather convinced me that
my wound was a flesh wound of the shoulder and
not serious.

Therefore I dismounted, stepped over to Sir
Hugh, disengaged his foot from the stirrup, and
tore the packet from his hand. His forehead and
the side of his face were covered with blood. He
was still breathing. Recklessly, I tore off a ruffle
from my sleeve and strove to stanch the blood. I
expected to see a round hole in the skull. There
was nothing there, however, but a deep gash that
extended sideways along the temple. I was not
skilled in gunshot wounds, but I realised instantly
that he was not mortally hurt, and I was never
more fervently thankful in all my life than for
that.

As soon as I saw what had happened, I took
my lace and linen tie and rapidly bandaged
the soldier's head. Then, as I knew I must get
away for my life, I mounted my horse again,

and, having first taken the precaution to detach from its straps a little despatch-bag that hung from the pommel of the saddle, I turned his horse's head back toward the inn and gave it a hearty stroke or two with my hand to set it galloping away. Thereupon, with a final and reluctant glance at the poor prostrate soldier, I put spurs to my own horse and galloped madly down the road, feverishly anxious to get away.

When I had got out of sight of any possible observation from Sir Hugh, even if he had recovered sufficiently to observe me, I turned my horse into the wood by the side of a little brook that crossed the road. I urged him through the trees until he was completely out of sight of any passerby. Then I swung myself from the saddle, tore open the package that Sir Hugh had handed me, hastily glanced over the papers, and discovered that the precious warrant was not among them!

Sick at heart, I hammered at the lock of the despatch-bag, which I thanked God I had had the wit to bring with me, until I got it open. It contained various official documents, and among them was one I recognised, to my great relief and happiness. Ruthlessly, I broke the royal seal. The

As soon as I saw what
had happened, I took my
lace and linen tie and rapidly
bandaged the soldier's head.
Then I knew I
must get away
for my life

name of my father swam before my eyes. It was the warrant for his execution.

With hands that trembled now as they had not trembled before during the adventure, I dragged from my pocket the flint and steel. Heaping together some leaves, touchwood, and dried brush, I soon kindled a blaze. I held the warrant therein with my hand and watched it burn. The wax melted at last and left a red spot in the middle of the ashes. I had succeeded, and by my own wit and address. My father's life was saved.

I had kept myself up till then by sheer strength of will. The wound in my shoulder had bled unheeded. I was greatly weakened. A sudden reaction came. I felt frightfully faint and ill.

I rose to my feet and managed in some way to divest myself of my coat and waistcoat, fumbling with my one hand amid the unfamiliar buttons. Then I tore open the breast of my shirt, dragged it off my shoulder, and discovered a long, jagged wound across the top. The sight of the red blood upon my white flesh made me nervous and sick.

I fell to my knees and started to crawl toward the brook. I did not know whether I should reach it or not. The world was growing darker and blacker about me every minute. I set my teeth together and crawled mechanically on. I had almost arrived at the brink when a voice I knew broke upon my ear, recalling me at once to full consciousness.

"Well, Master Carthew,"—the words came to me as if from a great distance,—"I have you now."

I looked up. There stood Sir Hugh, hatless, his head still bound, his cheek still bloody. He had a drawn sword in his hand. Amazing as it may seem, I was almost glad to see him: I felt so sick, and weak, and helpless. Yet I did not give up. With a flash of my old spirit, I strove desperately to rise to my feet. I got as far as my knees and, forgetful of my naked shoulder, I stared up at him boldly.

"Too late," I said.

"Good God!" I heard him exclaim. "'Tis a woman."

And then I knew nothing more.

Chapter

V

In which I ride away with my Captor, who threatens me with Death for High Treason

WHEN I came to my senses, I found myself lying in the arms of the soldier: that is, he was kneeling by me, with my head pillowed on his arm. It was a comfortable position, but I could not retain it a moment longer than was necessary. My wig had been pulled off; my face was wet with water from the brook, which he had dashed in it energetically; my throat was burning from some kind of liquor which he had poured down it.

After the first emotion of comfort from being thus supported, my immediate feeling was one of fierce indignation that he had so mishandled me. I opened my eyes and my mouth at the same time, furiously determined to protest. One does not come out of such a swoon, however, in full possession of one's powers, and in that particular Sir Hugh had the advantage of me, for, so soon as

I unclosed my eyes and before I had a chance to say a word, he spoke.

"My dear young lady," he began, with an air of masculine superiority which made me detest him.

That he should speak so to me was not to be borne. My weakness and faintness had passed. I resolutely drew myself away from him, and sat up. I maintained my position, too, although my head swam and things looked hazy and vague for a few moments.

"I am glad," said he with a gleam of triumph in his eye, "to see that you are better. Another swallow from this flask will probably put you to rights again."

He proffered me as he spoke a little silver-mounted bottle, which looked as if it might have been made to carry in the pocket. I shook my head positively.

"I want no more of it," I said. "I shall do very well as I am."

Then my eye fell upon my half-naked shoulder. With a convulsive movement, I swept my shirt across my breast, and held it there, and I know that my face was scarcely less crimson than the wound itself.

Sir Hugh Richmond, of course, saw my gesture. He paused, bit his lips to repress a smile, and then began resolutely.

" Madam," he said, as cold as you please, " I know not who you are, or why you have indulged yourself in this mad prank. You seem to be a gentlewoman. . . ."

Seem! Great Heavens!—and yet I was thankful for the acknowledgment after all, for goodness knows, there was nothing in my conduct which would indicate that I belonged to that degree.

" And, therefore, I beg to assure you that, until matters are explained to me and arranged between us, I regard you simply as a woman in distress, entitled to my respectful duty and protection."

" You are very kind," I said, seeing that he paused once again.

" It is difficult to say this," he resumed, with some little embarrassment, " but you have a raw and open flesh-wound in your shoulder. It is necessary that it be bound up. In the nature of things you cannot do it yourself. There is no succour or help within miles. You must allow me to act as your surgeon."

" Never! " said I.

" But the bleeding must be stopped," he continued imperatively. " You must be got away from here."

" I don't care, even if I bleed to death," I protested vehemently but most miserably.

" Madam, you must," was the stern answer. " In the first place, although I am loath to allude to it in your present condition, really you are now a prisoner in my custody. You have halted the King's messenger, robbed the King's post on the King's Highway. The act is felony; nay, more, 'tis treason. The punishment I pointed out to you a few moments since. I must convey you hence, and I cannot march you away with that open wound."

" Let me die here then! " I wailed, not realising that death was not imminent from that cause at any rate.

" 'Tis impossible," he said briefly, but with a firmness I could not stay. " And, in short, we have wasted too many words already."

He stepped toward me and bent over me. In my desperation I struck feebly at him with my unwounded arm.

" Madam," he said gently, catching me by the

arm, " surely you see how futile is your resistance
to me."

" But you are wounded yourself."

" A mere scratch," he replied. " Now, permit
me."

There was no help for it. I sank back on the
grass and hid my face with my right hand.
Never in all my life had I been so humiliated and
ashamed. The tears welled through my fingers.
I hated myself for weeping, but I had no power
to check their flow.

He whipped out a knife from some place, and,
with skilful hands, slit the shirt across my shoulder, laying it bare. For all my blinding my eyes,
I was acutely conscious of everything he did, and
a little thrill of admiration at his delicacy per-
vaded me. A ruder man might have opened the
shirt, but he took every care to conserve, so far
as was possible, my outraged feelings by exposing
me as little as possible.

" Have you anything," he said at last, after
he laid bare the wound and washed it with water,
which he brought from the brook in his hands;
" have you any bit of linen on your person with
which to bind it up ? "

" Naught," said I.

" If you only had a linen petticoat," he blurted out.

" Ay," was my answer. " If I had that I should not now be here wounded, helpless, and at your mercy."

He looked me over critically from head to foot. I could see betwixt my fingers. His glance, which was careless and indifferent enough, made my flesh fairly creep. Then he did a strange thing. He tore off his coat, and applied the knife to the sleeve of his own shirt. He cut it clear close to the shoulder, slit it in lengths, used the ruffles as a cloth to cleanse the wound, the edges of which he drew together, applied some plaster which he procured from a little box in his waist-coat, and then, with amazing skill and deftness, used the strips of his sleeve to bandage it all firmly and well. It is impossible to describe the relief afforded me by the process. When it was com-pleted, I drew down my hand from my face and looked gratefully at him.

" Now, madam," said he, " 'tis but a rough soldier's dressing, but the bleeding is checked, and 'twill serve until we can have it properly bandaged and attended to by a more skilful chirurgeon or apothecary."

There were a few small pieces of his sleeve lying by my side. I sat up and used them to wipe my tear-stained face and heavy eyes. Sir Hugh surveyed me thoughtfully yet most kindly while I did so.

" I believe," said he, " that, with my assistance, we can manage to get your waistcoat and coat on you. The wound is fortunately high up on the shoulder, and you can bend your arm with but little pain. I take it that you do not wish to be recognised as a woman, at least by chance wayfarers, and it will be necessary for you to make this effort."

" With your assistance, I am sure I can manage it," I said, rising to my feet.

He extended me a friendly hand during the endeavour, and I was very glad to take it. I was shaky still in my knees, but I had no doubt I could manage all that was necessary. It was an operation of some difficulty to get the coat and waistcoat on without hurting me too greatly, and indeed, although the pain was severe, I set my teeth together and it was presently managed. Next he mixed me a draught of spirit, well diluted with cool water, in the little cup around the bottom of the flask. After I had partaken of this,

I felt ready for whatever fortune had in store for me.

"You will be quite yourself in a few moments, I think. Meanwhile, I will allow you to rest at your ease while I inquire into this strange proceeding."

He indicated a fallen tree. I threw myself down on the grass and rested my head and unwounded arm upon it. Sir Hugh stood with folded arms by my side, quite in the attitude of a judge.

"Now," said he with ceremonious politeness, "that you are quite comfortable, will you kindly relieve my natural curiosity as to your extraordinary procedure?"

I hesitated as to how to begin the answer to this entirely natural request. Sir Hugh prompted me.

"First," he said, "it would be well for you to tell me your name and condition."

I could see no reason for concealing it. He had but to produce me in Edinburgh as his prisoner and a thousand people would tell him who I was.

"My name," said I, " is Katharine Clanranald."

The soldier started.

"What!" he exclaimed. "Are you the daughter of the Earl of Clanranald?"

"His only daughter," I returned.

"Lady Katharine Clanranald?"

"The same, sir."

"Is he your father whose warrant I was fetching from the King?"

"You speak truly, sir."

"The warrant; where is it?"

This was my one moment of triumph in all the interview now proceeding. I pointed to the remains of the fire off to one side.

"You will find what remains of the seal in that heap of ashes yonder," I said, smiling triumphantly.

Sir Hugh deliberately stepped over to it, carefully examined the heap of ashes, stirred it up with his foot, lifted the shapeless mass of wax in his hand.

"Your despatch-bag and the wallet you were good enough to hand me lie yonder," I said, "their contents otherwise intact."

He turned to them, picked them up, examined them carefully, thrust the wallet into the breast pocket of his coat, and turned to me, holding the despatch-bag in his hand.

" I see," said he, " that you have burned your father's warrant. Why did you do this, may I ask? "

" You were an enemy . . ." I began.

" Certainly not your enemy, madam," he interrupted quickly. " I simply serve my King and obey his orders. I have no personal feeling against you or against the Earl. That should be obvious."

" 'Tis a matter of indifference, your feeling toward me or mine," I replied coolly, at which he flushed darkly.

" May I ask what you expect to gain beyond delay by this most extraordinary action, which is fraught with consequences to yourself infinitely more serious than you can imagine? "

" I know to the full, sir, what are the consequences to myself, and, knowing them, I took the risk to save my father's life."

" But you cannot save his life by this means. It will be not difficult to procure another warrant, and your action has removed the last vestige of possibility of royal clemency. You have gained nothing but a brief delay for your father, while for yourself . . ."

" And that, sir," I returned, " is all that I de-

sire. New evidence hath been disclosed which
will be laid before the King, with application for
pardon signed by most of the great and loyal gentlemen of Scotland. I played for time. They
cannot execute my father without the warrant,
and, while one is being sent there, I shall be on
my way south to London, to plead with His
Majesty the Earl's cause."

"Humph!" said Sir Hugh, "you have for-
gotten one thing."

"And what is that, pray?"

"That you are now a prisoner attainted of
treason; that to-night I turn you over to the commandant at Edinburgh, and your place will be a
cell beside your father's. Two heads, one of
them a fair one, may go to the block instead of
one."

He spoke slowly and with cool deliberation,
which lent tremendous emphasis to every word he
said. I stared at him, bewildered, the truth of
what he said coming over me like a wave. Was
it indeed possible that I had risked everything and
to no avail?

"Sir, sir," I began, and then I hid my face in
my hands once more.

The pause was broken by the soldier.

" I never could abide to see a woman weep. The thought that many a hard adventure and many a bold attempt ends in a woman's tears has oft taken the joy out of some gallant undertaking," he said uncomfortably. " I pray your ladyship control your grief."

" Control my grief ! " I flashed out. " Put yourself in my place. I have staked everything, full of hope that I might thus insure my father's life, and you tell me that I have but made his death more certain."

" And have only involved yourself in his evil fortune."

" For that I care not."

" And there is no one for whom you care enough to regret this life? "

" None, save Master Dunner."

" Ah! " exclaimed Sir Hugh, " and who is Master Dunner, pray? "

" An aged retainer of our house, the attorney and councillor who hath aided me in this juncture."

" Was this wild plan his? "

" My own," I answered.

" And had you no man of your house to whom to turn? "

" We are alone, my father and I."

" And was there no gallant among your acquaintance who could relieve you of this desperate endeavour? "

" Not without a price greater than I could pay."

" And that price? "

I do not know why I answered these questions, but he stood before me so dominant and so masterful; I felt so miserable and weak and helpless; the enterprise which I had carried through so gallantly, and from which I had hoped so much, was apparently fruitless. I was as a child before him for the time being.

" The price, I ask," he repeated.

" Myself."

A slow smile swept across Sir Hugh's face.

" Have you never found that tall, strong, brave, true man, with bright hair and blue eyes; that brave, fierce soldier to all the world who reserves his tender side for you, who will worship you and think you as far above him as the stars, Master Carthew? "

" Not yet," I answered, bitterly ashamed of myself as he quoted my foolish remarks of the night before.

I looked pointedly at him as I spoke.

"My own hair is brown, my eyes and skin are dark." He shook his head sadly and then, with a swift change of manner, he continued, "But, do you know, I think I have found the woman of whom I dreamed, and of whom I told you over the cups last night."

There was a direct, not to say a burning, intensity about his gaze, as he fixed it on me, that fairly shocked me.

"I pray you, sir, do not mock me," I began in my confusion.

In spite of my words, there was something that thrilled my heart not only in what he said, but in the way he said it.

"I was never farther from mockery in my life," said Sir Hugh gravely.

"These," said I, "are the manners of the army, doubtless, which finds a sweetheart in every post."

"How admirable is your memory," returned the soldier.

"And 'tis most ungenerous to entreat me thus, being a woman, wounded, helpless, beaten, and your prisoner."

"It is so," said Sir Hugh contritely. "Madam,

you have rebuked me well. Now, what is to be done? "

It was obviously not for me to answer that question, so I remained discreetly silent while Sir Hugh pondered the situation, thinking deeply on his course.

" Do you know how far it is to the next town, Musselburgh I believe they call it? " he asked me at last.

I was tempted not to answer him. I would fain give no advice or counsel. I was not bound to give aid and comfort to the enemy. But lingering remains of discretion prompted me to placate my fierce conqueror by submissiveness, if possible.

" It is perhaps five or six miles by the road, I think."

" I could walk that distance easily. But you . . . We must get there some way. Once there, it will be easy to secure a conveyance to enable us to reach Edinburgh in safety. I see naught for it but to go to the highroad and wait the chance of a passing coach or wagon, which we will impress."

" My horse should be yonder," I said.

" I frightened him away when I came up."

" Your own horse? "

" You drove him off evidently, for when I came to my senses he was gone."

" We will go, then, to the roadway. How did you find me here, sir? " I asked, rising slowly to my feet.

" You left a trail that a baby could have followed." He smiled. " And, before we start, there is another matter that must be adjusted between us." He hauled out of his pocket as he spoke a netted purse containing the money he had won from me the night before. " This," he said, " is yours. I don't play at dice with women."

He extended his hand with the purse in it, and bowed low before me.

I took the money—oh, I did not intend to keep it! I was never so angered and humiliated in all my life.

" Surely, sir," said I, " I have some claims to be considered as having played the manly part in that, in broad daylight on the King's Highway, I have despoiled a royal messenger, a tried and proved soldier, of his charge, and, in an encounter at arms, have left him senseless in the roadway while I made off scot-free."

"You have described the situation and your action excellent well, madam, but this exhibition of manly courage, address, and daring does not make you less a woman. I may fight with you on necessity, but I cannot game with you. The gold is yours and you will have need of it," remonstrated the soldier.

For answer, I hastily flung the purse and its contents into the brook.

"Let it lie there," I said.

Sir Hugh laughed uproariously. Then he deliberately waded into the brook, fished up the purse from the shallow pool in which it lay, and put it in his pocket.

"Your true woman," he said, "flings away treasure; your true soldier gathers it up, that, at some future day, he may place it in her hand again."

"Lead on to the roadway," said I, as imperiously as you please.

"Had best cover your curls with the sunshine in them, madam, with your wig before we go," said Sir Hugh, lifting up wig and hat and presenting them to me with a graceful but most ironical bow.

I clapped them on my head in some fashion.

I was so angry that I neither knew nor cared whether they were rightly placed or not; and then, meekly to all appearances but with a heart filled with inward rage, I plodded through the forest to the side of the road.

Chapter
VI

In which, by the Favour of the King's Messenger,
I am permitted to ride south again on my
Quest

FORTUNE favoured us, for what should
come along but an empty coach and four
that had taken one of the minor gentry out
to his country seat and was returning to the city.
The coachman was sufficiently astonished at the
sight of a King's officer, his head bound up in a
bloody rag, and a pale slip of a boy in disordered
guise by his side. He halted instantly on being
hailed, and when Sir Hugh disclosed his name and
rank, and required the use of a coach to take us
to Musselburgh in the name of the King, he made
no demur, especially as his conscience was quieted
and any resentment mitigated by a guinea which
the soldier flung to him with a prodigal hand.

At his gesture, I preceded my captor into the
coach, and sank back in the thick cushions of the
seat with a great feeling of relief. Sir Hugh

clambered in after me, shut the door, and sat down by my side.

" I should relieve you of the annoyance of my presence," he said, " by riding on the box were it not for this unseemly appearance."

He pointed to his head, and my heart really smote me. I would have killed him I suppose to secure the warrant, if it were necessary, but I had no wish to see him suffer, thereafter. I was ever an impetuous woman, and at once I spoke my thought.

" Sir, you must be holding me strangely indifferent to one who hath so delicately entreated me, but I am ashamed to say that I quite forgot your wound."

" I forgot it, too," said Sir Hugh, " and, indeed, 'tis nothing to worry about. Had I water and a towel, save for a raw scar for a few days, there would be no evidence of it. I have had bullets into me and through me seriously and often enough to make nothing whatever of a trifling scratch like this."

" I thank God," I said fervently, " that it was only a scratch."

" Madam," he rejoined promptly, " you cannot be more grateful to Providence for that than

I am that my inadvertent bullet merely grazed your shoulder."

"Yet, sir, had you stricken me down, I had been saved from a worse fate."

Sir Hugh said nothing. The pause was almost unbearable. I broke it. He seemed to be waiting for me to do so.

"What . . . what is the punishment for treason?" I asked.

"The block, madam," was the sepulchral answer.

Now I was willing to die. Indeed, if my father had to die, I was more than willing. At least I had been until now. But there was something so sinister and horrible in the prospect my imagination conjured before me at his word that I went white and shuddered.

"'Tis a hard fate," said Sir Hugh swiftly, "hard fate for a brave man and harder for a sweet woman. There must be some way of avoiding it."

There was nothing that I could think of to say, no way that I could see for avoiding it, so I perforce kept silence, biting my lip, clenching my hands, and fighting back the tears that brimmed in my eyes in spite of myself.

" Madam," asked Sir Hugh, at last looking at me very hard, " have I not used you gently since the affair of this morning? "

" That you have! " I cried. " I shall not forget your kindness, your delicacy about . . . about my shoulder. A helpless maid could have fallen in no gentler hands. I shall thank you for your treatment during the rest of my short and unhappy life."

" Soldiers," said Sir Hugh, " are not always so black as they are painted. I am glad to hear you say that. I tried to treat you as I would a sister or a wife, had I been blessed with either. Now, will you allow me to question you on one or two points? "

" You may ask me anything, and anything that a woman may properly reveal I shall not keep back. I am glad to requite your services by entire confidence."

" You say that your father is not guilty of high treason? "

" No," said I, " I cannot say that, but I do say he went with Monmouth's adherents against his will; that he was in a measure compelled to, and that there are many circumstances which mitigate his offence against the King, so much so that, with the petition for pardon, we are persuaded that His Majesty will commute the sentence perhaps to exile or confinement."

" I am a soldier of the King, and, therefore, what I say may appear strange, but you interest me, madam. You interested me last night, you interested me more this morning, and you interest me even more at this moment."

If interest in his language did not spell some other word, then I fear I was no judge of hidden meanings.

" There is one argument to which the King is rarely insensible," he resumed rather guardedly.

" And what is that? "

" 'Tis heard in the ring of the guinea upon his fellow."

" We are not without some argument of that sort," I replied.

" And how much, pray, do your resources amount to? "

" About three thousand pounds, I think," was my answer.

" Including the hundred I won from you last night? "

He took the wet purse from his pocket and balanced it lightly in his hand.

" Including that," I said, humbly enough now in all conscience.

"Now, madam," he said, extending it to me once more, " I pray you as the good comrade of a poor soldier, who, although he hath been cozened by a woman, is not yet without some reputation, to accept this trifle as part of your father's ransom."

I hesitated. It was hard for me to put my pride in my pocket, but he had spoke me so fair and had treated me so well; his manner was so winning—and we needed the money so much—I actually took it.

"That's well done," he said, clapping me lightly on the shoulder, " and like a lad of spirit," he laughed.

I was unreasonably glad of his praise, I know not why; but honestly I set down my feelings as they came to me. I did not resent the friendly touch on my shoulder, either; its kindly animus was so apparent.

"You have been very good to me," I said, extending my hand.

He took it in his own firm, brown one, and held it strongly, yet without hurt.

" 'Tis the first lad's hand I ever kissed," he

laughed again, bending over it and pressing his lips upon it.

How different that from the pressure of Master Dunner's lips, or of any other that had touched my hand!

" I have put my pride in my pocket with my guineas," I said, " but what avail either now? I have simply succeeded in getting myself in prison with my father."

" There is many a thing happens between the arrest of a criminal and his being clapped into a cell," interrupted Sir Hugh, with a profoundly philosophic air. " But I have not yet finished my catechism, my lady. I asked you last night had you a sweetheart, and your confusion led me to believe that you . . . What am I to think now? "

" Sir," said I, " you have no right to question me as to my private affairs."

" No right certainly, but as a friend, as a possible ally, I still press for an answer."

" I have none."

" Answer or sweetheart? "

" Neither."

" And there is no gallant gentleman of Scotland to whom you are pledged? "

" Would I be here if there were?" I answered sharply.

" True," said Sir Hugh.

" Now it is my turn to question. Why do you ask?"

" Not idly, your ladyship, I protest. I have a good reason."

" What is that?"

" Your true soldier never gives his reason until he has to."

" Oh!" I remarked, indignant at being thus flouted.

" Nevertheless," said he, " I shall give you mine. I am willing to save you for yourself, not however for another man."

To save me! What could he mean? I stared at him, bewildered.

" I don't understand," I began.

" You will presently. Now, let me tell you something about myself. I haven't a relative in the· world, save a distant cousin, who would succeed to the title and estates should anything happen to me. As I hinted, I have admired and played with many women; I have loved none. I have never seen my ideal, whose qualities I prated of to you so volubly last night, until "—he paused significantly—" this morning."

" Oh, Sir Hugh! " I cried, " how can you thus make sport of my misfortunes? "

" I was never more serious in my life, madam, and I tell you this in order that you may understand my action and that consideration for no other person than yourself need obtrude itself upon my course. I intend, when we reach Edinburgh, to deliver you to . . ."

He stopped and looked hard at me, the conclusion hidden.

" The Lord Chief Justice," said I, completing his sentence. " It is just."

" To worthy Master Dunner, your attorney. I intend to place in his hands bills of exchange on my London bankers for the sum of seven thousand pounds, which, with your own three thousand, will better serve to move the King to grant your petition when you present it to him. His Majesty will be at Durham within a week. You can reach him there and save yourself the long journey to London."

I stared at the man in bewildered amaze, scarce at first comprehending the meaning of his easy sentences.

" But I am a prisoner," I faltered.

" My lady," was the answer, " you are as free as air. You can leave the carriage this moment, at your will, though I trust you will do nothing so precipitate and foolish as that departure would be."

" Then you don't mean to lodge information against me, and have me charged with treason, and imprisoned, and . . ."

" I mean to say . . ."

" But your failure to deliver the warrant? How can you . . ."

" That's easily explained. I was robbed by highwaymen, and . . ."

" But your honour, your reputation? "

" I think they will survive even such a strain," he continued easily.

" The seven thousand pounds? "

" I devote it to the service of your ladyship and your cause. The Earl, your father, can repay it at his convenience."

" And what," I asked, in my confusion, " hath brought me this noble, this most generous treatment from an enemy? "

" May you never have a worse enemy in all your life, Lady Katharine, than the one who now sits by your side."

The revulsion from despair to hope again was too great to be borne. When I realised the full purport of his words, I could scarce contain myself. I could find no words adequate to the situation. My usually ready tongue was paralysed. I knew not with what speech to break the silence.

"What hath so greatly changed you?" I inquired at last.

"You have," said the man bluntly.

I confess I liked the direct simplicity of the answer. Without giving me time for comment, he ran on:

"As I told you, I never saw a lad whom I liked better on short acquaintance than I did you last night. That you have turned out to be a woman in the morning, has only strengthened my"—he hesitated—"my regard," he added.

And, if that word did not spell what he had called interest had spelled to me before, again I was ignorant of the finer shades of meaning in the language.

"Never," said he, "in all my goings out and comings in through this little world, have I met a woman like you. I owe you a score which, I fear me, I shall never pay: that you, a mere girl, should have got the better of me, a tried soldier, fills me with shame and with admiration at the same time. I like your spirit. Should we have met under happier circumstances, it would have been my chief ambition to . . ."

He stopped suddenly. It was most annoying. I was burning to hear the completion of the sentence.

" To what, sir? " I asked. " Why don't you finish ? "

" Madam," said he meaningly, " as a soldier and a gentleman, I put no price upon my services to a woman;" whereat I was discreetly and deliciously silent.

It was noon when we rode into Musselburgh. Sir Hugh, making such excuse as would serve to justify our condition, ushered me into a private room of the inn with all the care and tenderness that my sex and helplessness merited. He left me to my own devices for a little space, and returned presently with a physician, the chief practitioner of the town. The doctor much marvelled, I doubt not, but questioned me not at all, because, as I afterward learned, Sir Hugh had warned him to make no inquiry as to what he saw. He sewed up the wound, re-bandaged it, complimenting the skilfulness with which it had been treated by the way, declared that I would suffer no great inconvenience from it, that it would be well in a short time, and left me.

After his departure, there was set before me the daintiest and most delicate meal, which I partook of alone, although, to be honest, I would have greatly enjoyed the company of my captor. I took occasion to freshen my face and hands, and lie down for a half-hour's quiet rest before Sir Hugh tapped on the door.

" How fare you, madam? " he asked, after I had arisen and bade him enter.

" Excellently well," was my answer. " I am greatly refreshed by the surgeon's visit, my meal, and this hour of quiet."

" Canst sit a horse, think you? "

" As well as ever in my life," I replied.

" Well, then, I have two here, and, if you are ready, we will ride."

Sir Hugh had bought himself a hat; the surgeon had attended to his wound—the white bandage about his forehead was not unbecoming to one of his soldierly appearance and bearing. He had made such explanations as were necessary, and, although there was quite a crowd about the door of the hostelry as we came forth and mounted our horses and rode away side by side, there was no demonstration.

We passed the time before we reached Edinburgh, riding slowly and being passed by several horsemen, in much pleasant converse, tacitly avoiding the subject uppermost in our hearts. Sir Hugh gave me much sage information about the King and how to approach him, for which I was deeply grateful.

His uniform and imperious presence procured us free entry through the gates, although it was well toward evening when we reached the town. Nothing would do thereafter but that he must escort me to my hiding-place. It was perhaps reckless and imprudent of me to allow him to have knowledge of it, but such had been his kindness to me that I could deny him nothing. I piloted him, therefore, by the back streets to the rear of our lodging. We tethered the horses to the fence and entered the house by the back way. Master Dunner, who had heard the clatter in the alley, met me at the kitchen door.

" Have you succeeded? "

" Beyond our wildest dreams," I said.

" Who is this? " asked the old man, peering back of me at the towering form of the soldier.

" This," said I, " is Sir Hugh Richmond."

" Good God ! " exclaimed the attorney, " have you taken him, my lady, as well as the warrant ? "

" Indeed," said Sir Hugh, laughing, " I think in truth she hath."

Chapter
VII

Wherein, at the Request of Lady Katharine Clan-
ranald, whom he loved, Sir Hugh Richmond
takes up the Tale, relating what happened to
him in the Tolbooth Prison

LADY KATHARINE CLANRANALD has
asked me to make this personal contribution
to her veracious narrative.

I shall not soon forget the mystification and surprise of worthy Master Dunner, counsellor-at-law.
I could well understand his amazement. That the
emissary of the King, presumably bearing the
royal warrant for his patron's execution, should appear at his carefully selected hiding-place in the
company of her ladyship was surely inexplicable.

His wonderment and admiration grew after we
had entered the dining-room and were seated
about the table partaking of the excellent repast
his worthy factotum had provided when, with
some promptings from me when she would fain
have minimised her own heroic part, the adventures of Lady Katharine were related to him. His

legal mind was quick to grasp the salient fact that
the warrant had been destroyed and that no execution could take place, therefore, until it had been
supplied by a new one. When this fact had been
thoroughly apprehended to his satisfaction, he had
time to give thought to other matters, and he proceeded to cross-question us both with a searching
power by which he learned everything that had
occurred.

" Why," he asked me, " did you determine upon
this quixotic action which would result in such
serious consequences to yourself, sir, were it disclosed to the King ? "

" Master Dunner," said I meaningly, " if the
good reason for my action be not apparent to you,
then all I can say, sir, is that you are a very blind
man."

At which her ladyship blushed divinely. She
looked charming as a boy, so winning, indeed, that
I could scarce imagine her fascination enhanced
by any change of apparel whatsoever, and I should
have kept her a boy forever were it not that I
could not see how in tha* capacity I could change
her name from Clanranald to Richmond, which I
was firmly purposed to do at the first convenient
opportunity, provided her consent could be ob-

tained, and of that I was bold enough to feel hopeful.

" Sir Hugh," she said, almost in answer to my unspoken thought, " I have to thank you for kindness so great that I know not how I shall ever repay you."

" I have rendered you some slight service, madam, a tribute to your gallantry and devotion, as one soldier might to another, and there is no word of repayment ever to be mentioned betwixt us," I said. " But now it grows late. I am expected at the castle to-night, I infer from what Master Dunner hath said, and it will be necessary for me to take my departure without further delay."

I drew forth from my pocket, as I spoke, the wallet of which my lady had despoiled me and which she had returned to me, and, asking for pen and ink, I gave to Master Dunner such writings as, in his judgment and mine, would enable him to command the sum of seven thousand pounds, which, with what he had, would complete the sum of ten thousand with which to approach the King. Master Dunner was very careful to give me such security as he could, acting as the Earl's agent and jealous for his patron's honour, and promised speedy repayment of the loan. Lady Katharine made some demur, but between us we easily overruled her: I, because I was determined that my quixotic impulse should be carried out; and Master Dunner, because he would have taken anything from anybody to save his patron. The transaction was soon over, and I arose to take my departure.

" I have a word of advice to give," I remarked, ere I said good-bye. " Whatever you do, do quickly. It is quite late. I may have difficulty in getting access to the Lord Chief Justice or the military commandant. Possibly I shall not see them until the morning. No messenger, it is likely, will be despatched to the King until late to-morrow."

" I will ride to the King myself early in the morning," said Lady Katharine immediately. " You told me that he would be at Durham by the time I could get there."

" Ay," replied I, " but it will be a hard ride for a woman."

" I will go just as I am," returned her ladyship.

" Your wounded shoulder? "

" A night's rest will put that to rights."

" Have you none other who can go ? "

" I have only two friends," returned her ladyship—and her appreciation really thrilled me—
" Master Dunner "—she hesitated—" and yourself, Sir Hugh," she continued, extending her
hand.

I do not know what made me do it. I had
kissed it in the carriage like a courtier. Now I took
her fine hand in my own and shook it well.

" As one soldier to another, lad," I said, clapping her lightly upon the shoulder for the third
time. " 'Fore God, I like you well, and, when
the time comes, I should be glad to have you in my
company," I said, with double meaning, " forever."

" Should I enlist as a soldier, Captain Richmond," returned my lady, saluting gallantly with
her disengaged hand, " I should like no better fortune than to follow your flag."

I dared not trust myself to continue the conversation in this vein. There was no doubt about
it, although I be writ down here as a fool, I was
head over heels in love with this beautiful and
daring woman. She had captured my heart as
completely as she had captured my person back on
the highroad. I was helpless before her. And

"*I like you well, and when the time comes I should be glad to have you in my company—forever*"

only the fact that she was in some small measure
in my debt prevented me from carrying her heart
by escalade. I would have taken it by storm
like a soldier had it not been that gratitude might
have inclined a capitulation, which I would not accept unless it came from an interest and affection
that equalled my own.

I answered her salute in kind, therefore, and,
not trusting myself to say another word, turned
on my heel and went out, accompanied by Master
Dunner, who desired to walk a space with me and
talk further about these various matters. He
begged Lady Katharine to retire at once and get
such rest as she could, if she persisted in her determination to ride south in the morning, and he
promised to be with her betimes.

" Sir Hugh," he began, as we walked along the
almost deserted street,—the house being in one
of the meaner quarters of the city for safety,—" it
is idle to attempt to disguise from me that you
have placed yourself in a position of considerable
danger."

" I did not choose," said I, " to dwell upon that
in the presence of her ladyship, for obvious reasons."

" I understand," said the old lawyer gravely,

and yet with a little twinkle in his eye. " Your
interest in her ladyship can only arise from one
cause."

" You are not so blind as I fancied, Master
Dunner," I returned, smiling. " I confess to you,
I have never met a woman of her spirit, her wit,
her resource, and, if I may judge from what I see,
of her beauty, of . . ."

" You may spare me the catalogue of her ladyship's attractions," said the old man drily, " not
because I am not fain to hear you dilate upon
them, but there are other matters more pressing
which must be considered between us, and more
interesting as well."

" There is nothing more interesting," said I—
and if I had been a young cornet instead of a veteran captain of horse well on his way to majority,
who indeed might have commanded a regiment
had he chosen to give up his place in the King's
bodyguard, I could not have been more reckless in
my speech—" than discussing Lady Katharine, but
what you say is true. I cannot and need not disguise from you that my position is somewhat
perilous."

" Exactly," returned the lawyer. " You have
been robbed of the King's warrant here in Scot-

land. The act is more than highway robbery; it is treason. The fact that the only warrant that is taken is Clanranald's points to some adherent of that house. It is possible there are those who will say that the resistance you offered was not so vigorous as you might have made, despite that bandage upon your forehead. You may have been observed. Indeed, I am sure you must have been, for you have admitted to me that you gave your full name and rank most imprudently at the city gate and at Musselburgh as well. Perhaps some one may have heard your conversation with Lady Katharine in the wood. In short, sir, I need not refrain from telling a soldier that you are in grave peril of being attainted for treason yourself as an accomplice—and, forgive me, that you certainly are—to a treasonable attack upon the King his privilege."

"Even so," I replied. " But I can honestly give my word that the warrant was taken from me by force, and back it with my oath were that necessary; that I did not surrender it willingly; that I did everything that I could to retain and defend it, and that it was not until I was senseless from a bullet wound that I lost it. I have not failed in my duty."

" Except," said Master Dunner, " you have not
given up to justice the assailant whom you captured after the assault."

" Lady Katherine? " said I.

" Exactly," was the answer.

" Well, my only defence for that is Lady Katharine herself."

" And how far think you would that go in a
court of justice? "

" Before a jury of soldiers, a long distance," I
laughingly replied. " But, jesting aside, I realise
all that you say, and, were any harm to come to
the King from my action, I should feel differently,
and I should have acted differently. Lady Katharine Clanranald made a brave play for a few
days' delay, and all I have done is to assure her
that she shall have the time for which she struggled. If the King persists in his determination
that the Earl shall pay the extreme penalty,
why, no great harm will have been done by
the few days' respite which he will enjoy. And
if, on the contrary, his daughter's enterprise
meet with its proper reward, a great harm
will have been avoided. Therefore, I justify
myself for what I have done, and hold it not
inconsistent with my honour as a man, my obli-

gation as a subject, or with my duty as an officer."

The reasoning was specious, but, specious or not, it had to serve.

" I am glad to see you in so reasonable a frame of mind," continued the advocate. " We are now upon the High Street. If you will refresh yourself in the inn yonder, I will have your horse brought to you and you can then ride to the castle and report to the Governor and the Lord Chief Justice while I turn these bills of exchange into drafts upon London. It would not advantage your cause, should you fall into difficulties, if I should be seen in conversation with you. But should you need an advocate, I recommend to you Master William Abadie, a skilled and learned counsellor-at-law, and my very good friend, through whom my own poor talent will also be at your service freely."

" I thank you," said I, " and I will await my horse here."

We parted with mutual expressions of esteem, and, though I have little affection for lawyers, I own I never met one that I liked better than Master Dunner. If I got in trouble and Master Abadie proved as agreeable, I should be in for-

tune.   I ventured to charge Master Dunner, ere
he left me, with a message of reassurance to her
ladyship, which he promised faithfully to deliver,
and I engaged his good offices as well to represent
my conduct to her in the proper light should occasion serve.

My horse was soon brought to me, and I made
my way without difficulty to the gates of the castle,
announced my name and rank, and demanded to
see the commandant without delay.   I was ushered
into the presence of General Ramesay.   He was
seated at a table in his office, and by him in another chair was another man of imposing, if somewhat legal, aspect.   General Ramesay received me
with a certain abruptness, which was somewhat
disconcerting.   However, I was not called to be
a censor to his manners, and, so long as he was
decently civil to me, I had no reason to make any
complaint.

I reported briefly that I had been stopped on
the road from Cockenzie to Musselburgh that
morning by a highwayman, with whom I had had
an encounter; that, although I had wounded him
in the shoulder, he had been fortunate enough in
an exchange of shots to strike me in the head;
that his bullet had laid me senseless in the road,

whereupon he had taken my despatch-bag, broken
it open, extracted therefrom the warrant for the
execution of the Earl of Clanranald, and made off
with it; that I had come to my senses, and, without a horse, had availed myself of such means as
presented to reach Musselburgh, where I had
bought the animal I had left outside, and I now
delivered my other despatches and reported myself subject to his orders.

General Ramesay heard me without interruption. When I finished my brief recital, in which
I told nothing that was not absolutely true, although I was very careful not to tell everything
that happened, it was the man on the other side
of the table who spoke. His accent was decidedly
Scottish. His manner was harsh, imperious, and
severe. I felt instinctively that trouble was to be
looked for from him. He had some notes scrib-
bled upon a sheet of paper before him, which he
drew closer and examined carefully through a pair
of great horn spectacles before he spoke.

" You lay last night at Cockenzie you said,
Captain Richmond? "

I turned to General Ramesay.

" Sir," said I, " I am quite willing, in the exercise of my duty, to answer any question, to obey

any order from you, my superior officer, but before I reply to this gentleman, will you kindly advise me as to . . ."

" This is Sir Alexander Forfair, Sir Hugh," said the General. " The Lord Chief Justice of Scotland. 'Tis he to whom the warrant was to have been delivered."

" I beg your pardon, your lordship," said I, bowing to the old man.

He wasted no time in ceremony.

" Your answer to my question, please."

Although I did not at all fancy his manner, and saw indication of trouble for me therein, I promptly replied in the affirmative with the best grace possible.

" You had as a companion at table a young "— he paused—" gentleman? "

" I had, sir."

" What was his name? "

" He told me that it was Carthew."

" Have you any reason for believing that that name was assumed for the occasion? "

I was silent.

The Lord Chief Justice was skilled in reading men, and he saw at once that he need press that question no further.

"He answers not, mark you, Ramesay," he said, turning to the General.

"Sir Hugh," said the old soldier, with whom I had some acquaintance, having served under him previously, "as a brother officer, and I may say as a friend, I advise you to be entirely frank with his lordship. You stand in a position of some peril."

"Pardon me, General Ramesay," interposed the other man. "We need not dwell upon that at present. Sir Hugh doubtless understands his position. He is experienced enough to know how grave it is and what the consequences of his refusal to answer would be."

I knew well how serious the position might be if these men knew all that I had done, but that they could know it was beyond belief. I determined, whatever might betide, not to betray Lady Katharine. I was in for it, I supposed, and I did not disguise to myself the gravity of the situation in which I had become involved.

"We know more," resumed Sir Alexander Forfair, "of your movements than you imagine, sir. We know that you and this young man were extremely friendly on last night; that you parted after an evening spent together on the most

amicable terms; that the young man left before
you did; that some sort of an encounter, as you
allege, took place in the wood a few miles this
side of Cockenzie. We know further that you
and the young man rode together in Lord Leven's
coach to Musselburgh; that you and he came a-
horseback to Edinburgh, and that you are now
here alone."

It was not difficult for me to see whence this information had come. My horse had gone back to
the inn at Cockenzie. The landlord had sent a
messenger immediately, who had observed the
blood and evidence of struggle in the wood. He
had galloped on to report the adventure to the
authorities at Edinburgh. They had been looking
for me. They had learned in some way of our
ride to Musselburgh, probably from the coachman, who would be apt to talk about it, and our
entrance through the city gates an hour since had
been doubtless reported.

What a fool I had been! I had permitted myself to be robbed by a woman and had become
so infatuated with her that the simplest precau-
tions had escaped me. I stood absolutely con-
victed. There was no defence I could make; no
explanation in the least degree plausible that I

could urge. In one moment the peril of the situation burst upon me. Lady Katharine's act had undoubtedly been treason. I stood as an abettor and participant therein. My only salvation would be to tell the whole truth and throw myself upon the mercy of the Justice and the King. If I did that, I had no doubt that I might escape with no more severe punishment than a reprimand. But that was the one thing I could not do. I had put my head in a noose, or under the axe rather, having previously fettered myself, hand and foot. I was helpless. What I should have been glad to have done for love of her ladyship, I had now the added incentive to do for my honour's sake. No gentleman, under such circumstances, could have betrayed a woman.

"Now, sir," continued the Chief Justice, as these thoughts ran lightning-like through my head, "what have you done with the royal warrant for Clanranald's execution?"

"It was burned," I answered.

"Who burned it?"

"The highwayman."

"And you permitted it?"

"I had naught to do with it, lying senseless in the road."

" Do you deny that the young man with whom you supped at Cockenzie and with whom, doubtless, you arranged this pretty little play was the highwayman ? "

" I deny nothing, sir, neither do I affirm anything, save that there was no arrangement between us; that I was assaulted upon the highway; that I made the best defence I could, and that I was wounded."

" Do you deny that you were thereafter this day in company with this young man ? "

A thought came to me.

" I will take oath, sir; I will pledge my word as an officer and a gentleman that I was not in company with any young man during the whole day, save such chance companionship as was thrust upon me by the inn-keeper at Musselburgh, the men from whom I bought horses, and so on," I protested warmly.

General Ramesay of his kindness here did me a good turn.

" I have known Sir Hugh Richmond these many years, my lord," he said to the Chief Justice; " we have served together and I would stake my life upon his honour."

" I have heard the testimony of many men,"

said Sir Alexander. " I think I am as able to tell when a man is speaking the truth as any judge in all Scotland. I beg to assure you, General Ramesay, and you, Sir Hugh Richmond, that I not only believe but know that you are speaking truthfully, for the man who held you up on the highway, with whom you rode to Musselburgh, with whom you entered the city, was a woman. What is her name? "

If a bombshell had exploded at my feet, I could not have been more amazed.

" That," I said at last, with such firmness as I could muster, " I decline to state."

" Sir Hugh Richmond," continued the old man, pointing his finger at me, " I rather like your bearing and appearance. I have no doubt what you say is, in the main, true; that you were robbed on the highway by a woman."

He laughed grimly, and, while I was willing to be robbed by her ladyship, I could have killed him for the mocking sneer in his voice. It is one thing to be robbed by the woman you love; it is another thing to be twitted about it and have the world throw the fact in your face.

But I could do nothing. It was part of the price that I would have to pay for the winning of her ladyship, which had become the chief object of my life, from the moment I held her wounded and senseless in my arms by the brook-side in the wood.

" But, sir," continued the Chief Justice, " while I, for one, am rather glad that the warrant hath not reached my hand, for I understand that a petition for pardon, with a full statement of certain circumstances which render it reasonable, is to be presented to the King, yet all this has nothing to do with your conduct. You are constructively guilty of the gravest dereliction of duty and of high treason, and it becomes my duty, sir, to see that you are arrested and tried forthwith. The fact that you have done this halfway under compulsion, and halfway out of foolish regard for a petticoat, or that which should have worn one I would better say, may mitigate your offence in the eyes of frail mankind, but the law takes no cognisance of that. I think, however, that I may promise you clemency and my interest with His Majesty, which is not small, as well, if you will disclose to me the name of your accomplice, the woman in question."

" That, sir," said I, bowing to the old man, " is the one thing which as a gentleman, if not as a justice, you will perceive that I can by no means declare."

"As a gentleman, sir, I am not discussing this matter, but as a justice."

"Then, sir," said I, "we have no common ground on which to meet."

"You may pay," said Sir Alexander, smiling grimly at my repartee, "for your silence with your head."

"At least, sir," I answered, "'tis better to pay with my head than with my honour."

"There is not a woman in Edinburgh," said my lord reflectively, "or in Scotland, that I know of, who could do this thing, unless it were Clanranald's daughter."

I was a veteran; I am glad to say I did not change colour or manifest the slightest emotion, although this arrow drawn at a venture had hit the mark.

It was General Ramesay who interposed at this juncture to relieve what might otherwise have been an embarrassing pause.

"She hath been searched for throughout Scotland. She hath vanished completely since her father's apprehension, and it is believed she is now in England," he said.

Would God she were, thought I.

" Well," said Sir Alexander, " whoever it was, she must be found. 'Tis not safe that such a woman should be at large."

He rose to his feet as he spoke and bowed grimly but not ungracefully toward me. Indeed I rather liked this stern old Justiciary.

" Sir Hugh Richmond," he said, " speaking as a man, and not as a justice, I will admit that there is some reason for admiration and protection and alliance with a woman of that stamp, if her person accord with her courage."

" Sir," said I, bowing in my turn, " her spirit is above all praise, and her wit and her beauty are beyond even her enterprise."

" I take it," continued Sir Alexander, " that if you escape the block, Sir Hugh, you will be a lucky man in more ways than one."

" Even should I not escape, sir," said I, " I shall count myself fortunate in what I have been able to do."

" As a man," continued Sir Alexander, stepping closer to me, " I offer you my hand."

I shook it heartily as he continued, turning to withdraw :

" And as a justice, if I have to sentence you,

it will be with a very grave regret. General Ramesay, with this information laid before you, attested by the landlord of the inn, the physician at Musselburgh, the soldiers on watch at the gate, Lord Leven's coachman,—you see we have agents everywhere and spies as well in these troublous times, Sir Hugh,—you will, of course, put this gentleman under immediate arrest, and keep him in close confinement, pending the formal presentation of the charges, the trial, and the King's pleasure."

After having thus boldly laid his cards upon the table and revealed the course by which our movements had been traced, and how he got knowledge that my companion was a woman, the Lord Chief Justice bowed to us both and left the apartment. General Ramesay summoned his guard, demanded my sword, placed me in ward for the night, allowing me to use one of the rooms of the castle upon my parole. At my urgent request, he forthwith sent a messenger for Master Abadie, urging him to come to me without delay. I was then left to my own reflections.

Well, I had done that which had brought my fortunes to a pretty pass, but, when I thought of Lady Katharine, I could not bring myself to regret it as I should. I had somehow a confident hope that Fortune, which had thus favoured me in permitting me to make her acquaintance, would be of service to her and see me through this coil of difficulty.

My head ached furiously, as it had off and on, from the wound, but I welcomed every pang with pleasure, for was I not suffering for her, and did I not know by intuition that she would be acutely conscious of every pang that I felt? Indeed, I think I was inclined to luxuriate a little in my martyrdom, and, although I was not base enough to declare the situation to Lady Katharine, yet I knew that she would hear of it sooner or later, e'en though I used every precaution to keep it from her.

Indeed, I realised that I must get word to her in some way of the fact that her venture was known; that my companion was discovered to be a woman, and that, if she wanted to get out of Edinburgh, she must do it that very night. Well it was for me that Master Dunner had given me the name of Master Abadie. It was through him that I must communicate with Lady Katharine at once.

Chapter
VIII

How I got the News of a noble Self-Sacrifice, how it affected me, and what I resolved to do for Sir Hugh Richmond

I NOW take up the telling of my own story once more.

Of all that happened as Sir Hugh has related it, I was, of course, in entire ignorance until some time after. He left me with a growing amazement and a growing admiration for his generosity. He had borne the humiliation of being overmastered by a woman with such good-humour and such gallantry that the shame an ordinary man would have felt in such circumstances was mine.

By not resenting it, he had laid me under a tremendous obligation, which he had increased until it was almost unbearable, by his after treatment: his refusal to take me prisoner, his risking his reputation and name as a soldier to shield me, his bestowal upon Master Dunner of the moneys which he had so generously offered to lend to my father in his strait, his advice and counsel as to

what was to be done.   Indeed, I could not with
my life repay what he had done for us, or to be
honest, not for us but for me, I thought.   Yet
I knew instinctively that I had it in my power to
bestow upon him a reward which, unless I were
greatly mistaken, would go far to compensate him
for all.

Under other circumstances, I would have considered his evident predilection for me, his admiration so boldly and yet so tactfully expressed,
as the mere casual compliment of a gallant soldier;
but his words were backed by deeds, and, strange
as it might be, I could not disguise the fact from
myself that the man's profession had been just
short of ardent devotion to me and my fortunes, of
passionate desire to have me for his own.

Was I willing or unwilling?   I had blushed
many times before during this adventure, but all
the colour rolled into one wave would not have
equalled the rush of emotion that came over me
when I put that question to myself and found but
one answer in my heart.

What a fool I was, to stand many a stubborn
siege and fall at the lifted hand of the first wayside comer!   And yet, how nobly he had behaved,
how gallantly he had treated me, with what self-

abnegation, with what generosity, with what infinite delicacy. He had shaken me by the hand like a man and called me his little comrade and clapped me on the shoulder and wished that I might be in his company. I admitted to myself that I could think of no sweeter command. If I were a fool, I even luxuriated and rejoiced in this my folly.

Although I was intensely weary from my two days of hard journeying, the emotions through which I had gone, and the strain through which I had passed, it was a long time before I fell into the sound and dreamless sleep in which I sought recuperation from all the fatigues and excitements of the days before.

I was awakened by the tapping of the serving-woman upon my door. When I made sleepy answer to her repeated summons, she said that Master Dunner was below and insisted upon seeing me at once, upon matters of the gravest import. I must hasten for life and death.

I thrust my bare feet into a pair of slippers, threw over my night-dress a robe which lay at hand, and descended the stairs to the dining-room. With Master Dunner was another elderly gentleman, at the sight of whom I started back in great dismay, for I would not thus be seen by any other than he who was as a foster-father to me. But the attorney stayed my intended retreat.

"This," said he, "is the learned Counsellor Abadie. You must waive ceremony and hear what is to be said."

Counsellor Abadie was a friend of our own advocate. I had often heard of him as one of the most eminent and upright attorneys of Edinburgh.

"This," said Master Dunner, "is Lady Katharine Clanranald, the heroine of the adventure of which I have told you."

"Madam," said the other attorney, bowing low, "I am vastly honoured to have the privilege of your acquaintance. As a friend and admirer of the Earl of Clanranald, your noble father, I want to thank you and congratulate you, in the name of Scotland, for your filial devotion and splendid courage."

"Sir," said I, "'tis but what any daughter might have done."

"But what few would have ventured upon," he answered.

"We are not here to exchange compliments— forgive me, Abadie," said Master Dunner impatiently. " Will you explain the situation to Lady Katharine? "

" Madam," said the other advocate, " I am charged with the delivery of an important message to you."

" From my father? "

" From Sir Hugh Richmond."

" No harm hath happened to him? " I cried in great alarm.

" None yet," was the answer, " but he hath been—er "—the advocate paused—" apprehended. He hath summoned me as his counsel, and he now desires me to say to you that it is known that he was in company with a woman disguised as a man; that the hue and cry is to be raised for you in the morning; that strict search is to be made, and that, if you have business which calls you from Edinburgh, you must get away to-night."

" What hath happened to Sir Hugh Richmond? " I asked.

" Why, nothing," began Master Abadie speciously.

" Sir," persisted I, now thoroughly alarmed, " I am my father's daughter. I am much beholden to the gallant gentleman you represent. I must know the whole truth."

" Tell her what she wants to know, Abadie," said my old friend sharply. " She is of the stuff that must know and that can bear."

I thanked him with a look.

" He hath been arrested, charged with dereliction of duty, giving aid and comfort to the King's enemies, high treason, in short," was the answer.

" My God! " I exclaimed.

" His whole course is known. It is believed, since he entered the city in friendship with you, that the robbery was arranged between you; that he was privy to it before and accessory to it afterward."

" But could he not say that it was I, and, by delivering me up, have saved himself? "

" Madam, he could not."

" Why not? "

" Can you, a soldier's daughter, ask that question? " returned Master Abadie. " His honour as a gentleman . . ."

" Oh! " I gasped. " Is that all? "

" All and enough, your ladyship."

" Is it known who . . . ? "

" Not yet. They seek a woman, not you especially."

" I will go at once and deliver myself up to

Sir Alexander Forfair and declare the whole story."

" But your father! " said Master Dunner. " The information must be spread before the King. We dare not trust the papers and the money to another hand."

" Was ever woman so torn," cried I, " between her father and her . . . ! "

I stopped. What was I about to say?

" Sir Hugh Richmond," interposed Master Abadie, " hath said that you are to give yourself no concern as to his fortune, but you are to go at once to the King. Some means must be found to get you safely out of Edinburgh before the morning. He bids you think not of him, but of your father."

" What is the punishment should Sir Hugh be found guilty, Master Abadie? "

" As he is a soldier," said the advocate, " he may have choice of being shot rather than be beheaded."

" I cannot sacrifice his life to save my father's," I continued, sick at heart and, I make no doubt, white to the lips at the dreadful alternative Fate had propounded to me. " I have no right to do so."

" Sir Hugh is an officer of the King's Guards,"
broke in Master Dunner. " They will not execute
him without royal approval."

" Ay," assented the other advocate. " General
Ramesay is his friend. They will not hasten the
procedure. I have his word on 't."

" But, if I surrender myself, they will let him
go free at once, and . . ."

" And your father, the Earl!" cried Master
Dunner.

" God help me!" I moaned.

" Ay, so may He do!" was the answer. " But
be advised by me, madam," continued my old
friend. " My brother advocate and I here have
talked the matter over carefully. The appeal for
your father must go to the King. The one chance
of clemency for Sir Hugh Richmond is there as
well. I tell you plainly that, even though you were
to give yourself up, which no gentleman could
suffer under any circumstances, his guilt in the
eyes of the law would be none the less plain. It
is not only your father's life, but Sir Hugh's as
well and your own liberty, that depend upon the
King's action; and the sooner you appeal to him,
the better it will be for you all."

There was sound sense in this certainly.

" Can I not see my father or Sir Hugh before I go?"

" It would be impossible," cried both gentlemen in a breath, " and fatal even if it could be brought about!"

" Can you get me out of Edinburgh at this hour of the night?"

" Ay," was the immediate answer. " Five hundred pounds hath bribed a soldier at the Dumfries gate. But it must be done within the hour or not at all."

" I have my clothes, but I shall need another horse?"

" It shall be here, it should be here now, for we have already taken order for it, anticipating your consent," answered Master Dunner. " How doth your wound?"

" I suffer nothing from it, the pain in my heart is so great," I said.

" 'Tis a hard fortune that drives you on."

" Hard indeed," said I, " but we cannot repine over that. The King fortunately is at Durham according to Sir Hugh's word. I should be there within the week."

" I would you had some one to ride with you!" cried Master Dunner.

"I had best go alone," I answered.

"But if you should be stopped in the way, Lady Katharine?"

"Think you," I cried, "that I have gone through all these perils and dangers to be stopped in the way?"

"Go and dress, then, and make you ready at once. I have here the petition, and something over ten thousand pounds in two equal bills of London exchange, easily carried and negotiable. You must do the rest," said Master Dunner.

"But hasten, I pray you, madam," added Master Abadie.

I nodded, turned, and ran from the room. I was soon dressed. Save that I donned a fresh shirt in exchange for that which I had worn, I wore the same attire as I had put on when I first set forth on the adventure. I do not suppose ever maid got into men's clothes quicker or more eagerly than I.

But for Sir Hugh, I thought as I fumbled nervously among the unfamiliar buttons, I would fain have been born a man myself. But now, in spite of my father's peril, in spite of Sir Hugh's danger, in spite of my own position, and the trying journey that lay before me, I could not but exult in this further and final evidence of my soldier's devotion to me, evidently as deep as it was sudden. I could no longer disguise, had I wished to, his feelings or my own.

When I descended to the hall, I found the two advocates waiting for me. Master Abadie, being able to ride a horse, was to accompany me as far as the gate. I bade farewell to Master Dunner, implored his prayers for my safe journey and success, and Master Abadie and I mounted our horses and rode quietly away through the deserted streets of the town. I heard the clock in the old church tower toll two strokes in the morning. There was no moon and it was very dark. None accosted or molested us. We were shrouded in horsemen's cloaks and went silently along, saying nothing.

The sentry at the gate was ready for us, and, faithful to his agreement, he slipped open the postern. I shook hands with Master Abadie, and then, upon the impulse of the moment, whispered a message to him for my soldier.

" Tell him," said I, " that I ride to the King to tell him all, to beg his clemency, and should I fail —he called me his comrade, we struck hands on it— I shall come back as a soldier to die by his side."

Chapter
IX

*My Interview with the King of England and the
good and bad Angels that attended him*

I PASS over the adventures of my journey albeit they were sufficiently thrilling to furnish pages for a romance. On second
thoughts I went via Galashiels, Hawick, Norham,
Warwick, and Shields to Durham. The distance
as the crow flies was not much more than a hundred miles; by the road it was perhaps half again
as long. I accomplished it in four days and a
half at the expense of a foundered horse which
I left at Norham. A man as hard pressed as I
could have done it in less time, I know, but for a
woman it was a fine ride, I have been told by those
whose judgment I value, and certainly it was hard
upon me.

Early in the afternoon of the fifth day my
horse and I staggered into Durham. Which was
the more tired I cannot say. For myself I was
utterly weary. What little good looks I might

have boasted in the beginning had been entirely worn away.

Had my errand been completed, I doubt not I should have collapsed utterly, but the hardest part was yet to come. I ascertained from the landlord of the hotel where I drew rein that His Majesty was still in Durham, or rather he was at Bishop-Auckland, the residence of the Lord Bishop of Durham. Rumour had it that His Majesty was to move on the morrow. I had no time to lose, therefore, and it was well that by hard riding, without sparing myself, I had arrived as soon as I had.

I was shown to a private chamber and there summoned the landlady and took her into my confidence. She was an honest, motherly sort of a woman. There was no reason for concealment. I told her who I was, and for what I had come, and asked her aid. She was blithe to assist me. I was well provided with ready money, not merely the bills of exchange for the greater sum, but sufficient for all the expenses of my journey, and it was an easy matter, therefore, for the worthy woman to procure me dress suited to my sex and station.

I lacked the freedom of my man's attire when

I was again stayed within my woman's garments, and yet there was a certain satisfaction in being once more a girl as Nature had designed me. I forced myself to partake of food and wine. The landlady and her daughter acted as my tire-women. Somewhat refreshed by my meal and a bath, I called a carriage, and accompanied by the young girl, set out in more comfort than at any other period in my journey for Bishop-Auckland.

I went just as I was, pale, haggard, drawn, and worn. With my short crop of curly hair I must have looked strangely out of mode. The landlady was for touching my cheeks with rouge and for supplementing my lack of long locks with false ones which she declared could easily be procured at the nearest wig-maker's, but I would have none of it.

It was quite late when we reached the castle, and some demur was made as to my admittance. It was not until I had declared my name and rank to the gentleman-in-waiting that I effected entrance. When I told him that I was my father's daughter, he looked at me curiously, but after a momentary hesitation bowed before me and led me into the palace, leaving the maid without.

I had never seen King James. The mean and

treacherous qualities he afterward showed, indeed, which were first displayed in his conduct after Monmouth's rebellion, had not yet become widely known, but we in Scotland had our suspicions of his character. I looked for no royal magnanimity or generosity from His Majesty.

It was with a dubious and a sinking heart, therefore, that I followed my guide. We presently stopped before a great door. The officer knocked thereon, and after a moment was bidden to enter. Directing me to remain where I was until further notice, he at once opened the door, and passed within, leaving it slightly ajar.

I had so much at stake that I did that from which under other circumstances I would have recoiled. I stepped closer to the door where I could hear what transpired, if I could neither see nor be seen.

" Well, sir," I heard a voice from within saying, high, thin, imperious notes, " what means this interruption? "

" May it please Your Majesty," was the reply, " there is a young woman without who seeks audience."

" Woman! What woman? " the first voice ran on.

"She says that her name is Clanranald, Your Majesty."

"What!" came in violent suddenness from the one whom I judged to be the King.

"Yes, Your Majesty. She professes to be Lady Katharine Clanranald, daughter of the earl of that ilk."

"What would she with us? We will not see her."

"A woman," broke in a third voice, harsh, cold, infinitely brutal and cruel, "Your Majesty, should ever be welcome to a king, especially if she have no natural protector."

How I loathed and hated that voice with its frightful insinuation! I wondered whose it might be? But I had no time to indulge my emotions, for the King spoke again.

"True," he laughed, "Clanranald must ere this have left his head by the block. Sir Hugh Richmond hath had time to go and come."

"Those," said a fourth voice, "who are father-less should have a father in the King, Your Majesty."

It was in substance just what the other man had said, but how different was its tone and meaning? There were sweetness, gentleness, as well as force in the new voice that moved my heart. There was some kindness in that room then after all, I thought.

"Well put, my lord," said the King. "Captain Culver, you may admit the lady."

"How," said the third voice, which had made the ineffably brutal suggestion a moment before, "if she be armed and hath come to revenge her father's death?"

"Well thought on, my lord," said the King.

"I will take it upon myself to see that Your Majesty comes to no harm," broke in a fifth voice at this juncture, speaking our language brokenly with a slight French accent, by the way, which I shall not attempt to reproduce.

"'Tis well, my friend. Stand you there on guard with your sword drawn and keep the girl at a distance."

"I want no sword, Your Majesty," was the reply, "to master a woman."

"I hold you responsible for her, Louis. Now, Captain Culver."

In another moment my messenger and guide came out to the anteroom, threw open the door, and motioned me to proceed. Summoning my courage, I stepped through the doorway. The

door was closed behind me immediately, and I
found myself in a vast vaulted room, a library
apparently. On a high chair at the head of a
large table sat the King. I knew him at once. To
his left there was a man in the robes of a Bishop
of the Church, a man of kindly, benignant, gentle,
merciful face, so different in his aspect from the
man who sat on the other side of the King that
his good heart, which would have been evident
anywhere, was the more marked by contrast. The
other man wore the dress of a cavalier, but he
had thrown over it the robe of a justice. His face
was handsome but marred by the most brutal,
cruel, and licentious expression. His eyes stared
at me and his look was an insult. On the hither
side of the table an elderly but gallant soldier of
foreign aspect in the rich uniform of a general
officer waited. Next to the Bishop's his was the
pleasantest countenance that I fronted. Pride,
haughtiness, cruelty, covetousness were evidenced
in the King's face, but by the side of the man
next to him, he almost looked like an angel of
light.

I surveyed the four with lightning-like rapidity.
I was fighting for life, my father's life, Sir Hugh
Richmond's life, and I almost felt in that baleful

royal presence for my own honour as well, and I must take stock of my enemies or friends.

"The King, madam!" cried the soldier, inclining his head toward His Majesty as I advanced.

I sank to my knees instantly and stretched out my hands.

"Your Majesty," I pleaded, "mercy!"

"Rise, madam," said the King. "Nay, stand you there," he added quickly as I rose and made a sudden movement toward him, "by the Earl of Feversham."

I glanced rapidly at the soldier. So this was Louis de Duras, the French soldier of fortune, the favourite of the King, the commander of his armies, the hero of Sedgemoor. This was the commander who had dashed all of Monmouth's hopes. It was the Bishop who spoke.

"Your Majesty, the young woman looks weary. Will not your grace permit her the privilege of a chair?"

"Ay," said the King indifferently, "she may be seated, if she will."

"I would make the rebel stand," growled the man upon the other side under his breath while the Earl of Feversham courteously handed me a chair.

" I' faith you have made many of them stand upon nothing, Jeffreys," laughed the King uproariously.

So that was Jeffreys, he of the Bloody Assize, the greatest disgrace to justice that ever had been seen in all England. He had hanged and burned and beaten and scourged and robbed and murdered without let or hindrance after Sedgemoor, and writ his name in such gory letters upon the pages of history that not all the waters of all the oceans could ever wash him clean, or wash out his damnable record. I looked upon him and I hated him.

The fierce soldier, the unjust judge, the mean king—into what den of wild animals had I thrust myself? Well, I had played gallantly heretofore, and I would bear myself in the same way to the end.

" I thank Your Majesty," I said, declining the proffered seat. " I come as a suppliant from my father."

" From your father?" inquired the King in great wonderment.

He looked at Jeffreys and laughed.

" You must have come from hell then," roared the Justice, emboldened by the King's look, " for

the vile traitor's head hath rolled from the block
four or five days since."

" Shame ! " murmured the Bishop, not so low
but that all could hear.

I despised Jeffreys; I loathed him; I answered
him back not as a woman, I am glad to say, but as
a man.

" That's a lie ! " I cried impetuously. " My
father lives."

" The falsehood can easily be made truth then,
woman ! " cried the King, leaning forward with an
angry frown.

" At Your Majesty's pleasure," said I boldly.
" God hath put the lives of your poor subjects
into your hand, but it is to stay that royal hand
that I am come."

" What mean you ? "

" Give me leave, Your Majesty," interposed
Jeffreys. " A royal warrant for the execution of
the Earl of Clanranald was made out; I wrote
it myself. It was sent to Sir Alexander Forfair,
my brother of Scotland. Hath he dared to delay
its execution, hussy ? "

He rose as he spoke, leaned over the table and
shook his fist in my face. I cannot describe the
insolence, the overbearing brutality of his man-

ner. I looked him straight in the face, and answered nothing.

" Well, madam? " cried the King.

" Your Majesty," I answered, " I will hold no converse with this man. My errand is with yourself."

" Give her to me, Your Majesty," roared Jeffreys. " I will have her stripped and whip her naked at the cart's tail like Anne Lisle and the rest of the cursed brood of rebels."

" Sire," interposed the Bishop quickly, " Your Majesty will not do this thing. The meanest subject hath the right to appeal to the Crown, and here is a defenceless woman who begs only for her father's life."

" Peace, Jeffreys! " said the King. " As for you, my lord of Bath and Wells "—so this was good Bishop Ken of whom I had heard!—" your advice for once is good. I will hear the lady. Madam, your story."

" I thank Your Majesty," I said quickly. " Sir Hugh Richmond was set on by a highwayman near Edinburgh, shot, left senseless in the road, despoiled of the royal warrant, which was burned. Therefore, there hath as yet been no execution, fortunately for my plea."

" The matter then is but postponed," said the King indifferently.

" For the present, yes, Your Majesty, but meanwhile if Your Majesty will permit me "—I took from a little bag which hung at my waist a parcel of papers—" here is an appeal for clemency. 'Tis signed by the Lord Chief Justice and the Justices of your High Court. 'Tis countersigned by many great and loyal gentlemen to Your Majesty. 'Tis attested by depositions to show my father's unwillingness to follow the Duke of Monmouth, his efforts at restraint. Upon it I base an appeal for mercy."

The King looked hard upon me, frowning as before.

" Fetch hither the paper, Feversham," he said at last.

When it was placed in his hands—it was a brief paper for all its weighty import—he glanced at it curiously and balanced it a moment, his eye turning to Jeffreys and then to Ken. What was passing through his mind? I divined instantly. He would give it to one or the other of these men for examination, and as he gave it, he would determine the fate of us all, for I do believe no human soul ever looked to Jeffreys for mercy and received it.

My hand caught my throat. I bent forward, such pleading in my looks as for the moment seemed to move even the hard heart of the King. To my relief, he turned to the left and handed the note to the Bishop.

" Do you examine this, my lord," he said, " with all speed, and let me have your best opinion of its contents."

Ken instantly opened the paper.

" Now," said the King, turning his face toward me, " while my lord of Bath and Wells reads your humble petition for mercy, I would fain question you further, madam."

" I have naught to conceal from Your Majesty," replied I.

" You say that Sir Hugh Richmond was stopped and robbed in the highway? "

" Yes, Your Majesty."

" Was he seriously wounded? "

" No, Your Majesty."

" Why hath he not returned at once then to report the failure of his errand? "

I hesitated.

" Sire," said I at last, " rumour hath it that he is under close arrest."

" Arrest! "

" It is suspected that he connived with the highwayman."

" That's treason! " roared Jeffreys.

" But, Your Majesty. . . ." I faltered, and
then I stopped.

How could I say that it was not true, for it was.
The King looked puzzled.

" Hath search been made for this highwayman ? "

" I suppose so," was my answer.

" Your Majesty," interposed Feversham, " I
know General Ramesay well. He would leave no
stone unturned to apprehend the villain who affected this bold despoilment."

" Evidently," said the King to me, " it was some
one interested in the welfare of your house who
thus robbed my messenger on the highway. Do
you know his name? "

What I did from one point of view was wild,
foolish, reckless, and yet I believe that my action
was the result of one of those sudden inspirations
which sometimes govern people to their weal or
woe in critical moments.

" Your Majesty," said I boldly, " I myself despoiled your messenger."

" Good God! " exclaimed the King, " you, a

woman, to overmaster a tried soldier like Sir Hugh
Richmond?"

"It was not as a woman that I did it."

"What mean you?"

"In man's attire I won his friendship, Sire, and
then unsuspecting shot him. My bullet fortunately,
however, glanced across his forehead and merely
stunned him. His bullet tore its way through my
shoulder."

"Here is no collusion between ye then," said
the King.

"Nay, Your Majesty. But afterward when I
had burned the warrant, Sir Hugh overtook me,
discovered me to be a woman, had compassion on
me, failed to report my assault, did not deliver me
to the authorities, and now languishes in the Tolbooth in my place."

"That accounts for your short hair," said the
King irrelevantly. "I had wondered why you
came thus out of the mode. You cut it off to pass
for boy?"

"Your Majesty's penetration does you high
honour," said I, passing him the sweet compliment deftly.

"I should like to see thee as lad," laughed the
King. "What think ye, Jeffreys?"

" Saving your grace," cried the Justice, " I think her an impudent, traitorous wench who deserveth nothing whatever from Your Majesty's hands but a place on the block beside her father and her paramour."

" You coward! " I cried. " You low, base, ineffable cur! "

" Did ye not pay a price to Sir Hugh for his complacence, answer me that, you little baggage? " he roared.

" Your Majesty," cried I, flaming, " I appeal to you as the first gentleman of your kingdom to protect me from the insults of this man. Naught, I declare upon my word of honour as my father's daughter, hath passed between Sir Hugh Richmond and myself that the whole world might not know."

" You go too far, Jeffreys," said the King, turning upon the Chief Justice. " This passeth even my easy permission."

" I shall be pleased, madam, with the King's gracious permission," said Feversham with the chivalric gallantry of his race and ancestry, " to make your cause my own."

He touched his sword and looked threateningly at Jeffreys. There was kindly blood in this courteous soldier. I thanked him by a grateful look. It was the good Bishop who interposed in the angry scene.

"Your Majesty," he said, "I have read here the papers. 'Tis as the maiden declares. The petition is signed by the most noble and most loyal gentlemen of Scotland. The affidavits indicate the Earl of Clanranald's reluctance, his endeavour to restrain his fellow-conspirators. Here is surely a case for clemency."

"Did you ever see a case that was not for clemency?" roared Jeffreys.

"Few indeed, sir," said the Bishop, confronting him without blenching.

The King took the papers and stood looking at me thoughtfully. He was hesitating. With a prayer I played my last card.

"Your Majesty," I said, "out of the wreck of my father's fortune I have here some five thousand pounds, which should Your Majesty incline to mercy, I will gladly place in Your Majesty's hands."

"Bribery, woman!" cried the King.

But I had wit enough to see the answer.

"God forbid, Your Majesty, but there must be some worthy friend, some needy charity which

Your Majesty would be glad to relieve with this
benefaction and evidence of our gratitude."

"What would you do, Jeffreys? The maid
speaks fair."

"Were I the King," growled the Justice, "I
would have the head of the Earl, the five thousand
pounds, and the woman as well."

"And your advice, Lord Bishop?"

"I would give the maid her father's life, her
own liberty, and return her the five thousand
pounds."

The King paused.

"I choose the middle course. She shall have her
liberty and her father's life, and we will keep the
five thousand pounds . . . for charity, my
lords."

Chapter

X

*In which I bargain successfully for that which is
as dear to me as the Life of my Father*

I HAD succeeded in saving my father's life. It
was incredible, but none the less true. Yet my
task was but half achieved. All my joy would
be turned into bitterness, if, through my action my
good friend, Sir Hugh Richmond, were to suffer.

"Make out a pardon," continued the King,
"for the traitorous Earl of Clanranald. Let it
be conditioned upon his instant departure from
our realm of Scotland. If he be found alive
therein four days after he hath been enlarged from
prison, his head shall be forfeit. Make out also
a safe-conduct for this brave young lady back to
Scotland."

The King spoke directly neither to the Bishop
nor to the Justice. It was Jeffreys who broke the
silence.

"Do it thou, Lord Bishop," he said roughly.
"Thy hand is more used than mine to the writing
of pardons."

" Thank God for that! " said the good Bishop, drawing writing materials toward him and at once beginning.

" Art satisfied with our royal clemency, madam? " said the King, smiling.

" Sire," I replied, " it fills me with joy, but 'tis only what I might have expected from your royal mercy."

May God forgive me for that atrocious lie! I whispered the instant I had uttered it, as I continued:

" I have yet another petition to lay before Your Majesty."

" What's that, girl? " said the King. " Hast another father? "

" Not a father this time. A lover, as I live! " roared Jeffreys triumphantly. " Said I not so, Your Majesty? "

" Not a lover," said I to the King, " but Sir Hugh Richmond lieth charged with treason under close arrest. I would also have a full pardon for him."

" Pardon for a traitor? "

" He is not so guilty as he seems, Your Majesty. I robbed him of the warrant fairly and burned it. It was not until after it had gone that he retook

me, and then his treason consisted in letting me
go free that I might appeal with confidence to
Your Majesty's tender heart."

The King swelled visibly.

" Ay," he said, " tenderhearted should be the
King. My lord Jeffreys, did any one ever attribute
tender heart to you ? "

" Not in the service of Your Majesty," bellowed
the Justice. " I have no heart to pity treason to
Your Majesty."

" ' Blessed are the merciful,' " interposed Ken
softly, " ' for they shall obtain mercy.' "

" Mercy," said the King, who was in a tender
mood apparently, " 'tis a pleasant word."

Indeed he might well think it so, since by common report it was one he was but little accustomed
to use.

" Out upon both word and thing! " cried Jeffreys. " I plead for justice on the traitorous soldier. Your Majesty's power hath been limited
already by the mercy you have shown the false
Clanranald."

" ' And earthly power doth then show likest
God's when mercy seasons justice,' " quoted the
Bishop still softly, looking kindly at me.

I recognised Master William Shakespeare's

words as I had recognised them before on Master Dunner's lips.

The King hesitated as before between these two differing counsellors. And once more I threw the golden weights in the balance, hoping to incline it my way.

" If it please you, Sire, I have yet another five thousand pounds. . . ."

The King started.

" For charity, Your Majesty," I added quickly, " if Sir Hugh Richmond be enlarged."

" By the Mass," said the King, betraying himself, at which Ken started, " methinks the lady rains gold pieces."

" Sir Hugh Richmond's whole estate will be confiscate, Your Majesty," said Jeffreys. " 'Tis worth much more."

" Why, so it will," replied the King, " yet five thousand pounds more for charity, 'tis a goodly sum, hey, my Lord Bishop ? "

" Indeed, Your Majesty, well expended it will relieve the suffering of many of God's poor," returned the Bishop.

" Quite so," said the King.

He stopped again. I had played my last card. I could do no more if it failed. Jeffreys opened his mouth to speak. As he did so, my heart sank, but the King stopped him.

"My Lord Chief Justice," he said, "we will decide this matter ourselves. Madam," he said at last, "your plea for mercy hath been heard again. Sir Hugh Richmond's life shall be spared. His estates shall be confiscate. He is broke from his rank, dismissed from our guards, and must leave our realm at once. My Lord Bishop, since you have already tried your hand, will you draw up the writing for that?"

"With alacrity, Your Majesty," said the Bishop, busying himself writing once more.

"Now, madam, I believe that all is completed except . . ."

The King paused.

I thrust my hand into the bosom of my dress and drew forth the bills of exchange. I very well knew what he wanted; the mean King, not content with confiscating my friend's estate, would have the bribe as well. He was more avaricious even than the base and contemptible Jeffreys if it were possible for any one to go lower than this unjust judge.

"They are here, Your Majesty, ten thousand pounds in bills of exchange upon London," I said, lifting them up.

" You may present them yourself, madam," said
the King with a manner he meant to be gracious,
as I made as if to hand them to General Feversham.

Thereupon, I approached the King, taking care
that my access to him should be on the side of
Bishop Ken, who drew back courteously as I came
near. I knelt before the King and extended the
papers. His Majesty took them, examined them
cannily, laid them on the table before him, and
extended his hand. I had just bought his favour
in the most barefaced and open way, yet such as
it was I had received mercy, although I knew that
without the money, all my pleas would have been
of no avail. There was no help for it; although
I could rather have bitten it, I had to kiss the
royal hand.

" Here are the writings, Your Majesty," said
Bishop Ken.

The King signed them; they were sealed with
the royal seal which lay upon the table, folded,
tied, waxed by the Bishop's own hand, and then
were handed to me. I had triumphed in all points.
I could not resist a look at Jeffreys as I took them.
And if looks could kill, he had been a dead man.
Indeed, for that matter, my lord repaid my en-

venomed glance with interest. I little knew what was brewing behind his malevolent aspect.

"Here, too," said the King, "is your safe-conduct."

"I thank Your Majesty once more," said I, "with all the gratitude in a daughter's heart, and now I crave leave to withdraw."

"Wait!" cried Jeffreys hatefully. "Your Majesty, you have pardoned two notorious criminals, one an atrocious rebel, the other a traitor against your person. You have not, however, disposed of this woman."

"What mean ye, Jeffreys?"

"By her own confession she, too, is a traitor to Your Majesty. She robbed Sir Hugh Richmond on the King's Highway. She burned the warrant for her father."

"Shame!" protested the Bishop, rising. "This passeth all bounds, Your Majesty. I have kept silent while this bloodthirsty Man of Belial hath raved and blasphemed. Were I not a man of peace . . ."

"I wear a sword as I have said, Your Majesty," interposed Feversham, "and I will most gladly make this lady's cause my own if you will but give permission."

" Peace, gentlemen all! No brawling in our presence. My Lord Chief Justice hath spoken true. This woman is a traitor, and we have not yet disposed of her personal affairs."

I would have given the world at that moment for another five thousand pounds.

" Perchance," sneered Jeffreys, almost, as it were, reading my thoughts, " she hath come prepared with another offer to Your Majesty's needy charities. Is it so, madam? "

" Alas, sir," said I, lifting my hands, " you have my all. My only hope is in your clemency."

" You shall not hope in vain," said the King promptly and to the great surprise of everybody, I am sure.

" Thank God that I hear Your Majesty speak those words," cried the Bishop.

There was a muffled roar from Jeffreys.

" Is she to go scot-free, Your Majesty? "

" No," said the King. " Her punishment shall be suited to her crime."

What could that be, I thought, but death? Well, if I had saved my father and Sir Hugh, I could well die.

" I will confer," said the King, " with the Bishop here upon it."

At that my hopes took an upward bound.

"But first," he turned to me again, "I would have you return to your abiding place and after supper present yourself to me as the highwayman you have declared yourself to be. Meanwhile leave here the papers."

"Sire!" cried I imploringly.

"Enough," said the King. "My mind is made up as to that. Feversham, do you escort this lady. I hold you responsible for her custody. She must be produced here after supper, and mark ye that she come in manly fashion else she shall feel the weight of our displeasure."

"May I not have my father's and the soldier's pardons to take with me?"

"They shall be delivered to you to-night," was the unsatisfactory reply.

My heart sank. Perhaps some of my disappointment appeared in my face.

"On the word," said His Majesty, "of a king." He paused as if there were some doubt as to the value of that attestation, as indeed there was. "On the word of a gentleman, I promise you shall have them," he added.

He bowed not ungracefully. He had some of the Stewart charm, for all his meanness, when he chose to display it. He picked the pardons up and handed them to the Bishop.

" Here, my lord, do you be the custodian of them until the lady returns."

" I would Your Majesty had given them to me! " cried Jeffreys.

" I know you too well for that," laughed the King.

" You have played at mercy, Sire," said the Justice, frowning.

" It was my fancy," said the King haughtily, " for the first time; it may be for the last time, but whatever it be, I will not have it questioned. Go, Feversham. Until to-night, madam. And you, my lords, attend me."

The Earl of Feversham, who had evidently been deeply moved by my story, was kindness itself to me. His own carriage, a much more luxurious equipage with much better horses than the public conveyance I had hired, which he dismissed forthwith, was placed at my disposal. Together we rode back to the inn, and taking my word of honour that I would present myself in the parlour thereof in due time to enable us to keep the appointment with the King, he most obligingly left me to my own devices.

Bidding the inn maid who had accompanied me to call me without fail in time for me to make ready, I slipped off my dress, threw myself upon the bed, and fell instantly to sleep. The greater anxiety had been removed from my heart. Although I do not pretend to disdain life, yet since I had secured the freedom and immunity from further punishment of my father and my soldier, naught else very greatly mattered. I did not really think that anything very serious was toward, so far as I was concerned, and whatever may be the explanation, I fell fast asleep. The short period of rest greatly refreshed me and presently I felt another woman.

When the maid summoned me, I arose, bathed and put on my faded, tarnished suit of blue and silver. Round my waist I belted my sword, freshening the clothes where I could, and then booted, spurred, wigged, hatted, coated, armed, I descended to the parlour where the Earl of Feversham awaited me. He was evidently much struck by my appearance, but had the delicacy to say nothing.

We returned to the palace a-horseback, it being quicker and suited to the changed conditions. Promptly at the appointed time we were ushered into the presence of the King in the same room in which the interview of the afternoon had taken place. Now, I had worn this suit of blue and silver after the first compunction of conscience with absolute indifference. I had become entirely accustomed to it, and my modesty took no affront because I was seen abroad in it. I had passed muster easily enough for a stripling and I had never thought of what the clothes concealed or revealed until that moment when I stood in the presence of the King.

The same gentlemen who had been with him before were with him now, Jeffreys on his right, Ken on his left. Naturally I suppose I made a striking figure. Their curiosity was, without doubt, much excited, and they were all anxious to see me. The look that the Bishop bent upon me was full of interest, but it was full of a gentle consideration, almost of pity. He might have looked at his own daughter that way, deprecating the fact while he acknowledged the necessity for her unmaidenly appearance. But the glances of the King and his minion were so brutal, so suggestive, so degrading that unconsciously, as my face flamed and my body tingled, I clapped my hand to the hilt of my sword.

"By the Mass," laughed the King, although there was a quaver of uncertainty in his cowardly voice, "never lay your hand on your sword in the royal presence in that manner. Stay, madam," he cried hastily as I made a bold step forward. "Feversham!"

The officer quietly laid a restraining hand upon my arm.

"Bethink you where you are, madam," he whispered, "and how much depends on your conduct."

"Your Majesty," said I quickly, "I did but lay my hand upon my sword to proffer it in your service,"—which was another falsehood, for I would have been glad to have driven it into Jeffreys' black heart in his very presence; ay, even into the King's heart also.

"You come of a stock, madam," said the King, "which makes us doubt such protestations of true service. Yet she can be a bold enough enemy; hey, my lord?"

He turned to the Bishop.

"She hath shown here, Your Majesty," returned the prelate, "how deeply devoted she is to the noble earl, her father."

"She shows more than that," roared Jeffreys,

leering lustfully, " she shows a pretty figure, a well turned leg. . . ."

My hand went to my sword again. Had I been a man, I could not have more fiercely resented his disgracefully insulting words and looks. Again Feversham laid his hand upon my arm.

" Sire," he burst out, " this is unendurable. Your Majesty hath made me the protector and guardian of this lady. As a man of the sword I usually have little to do with those of the robe, but on my word . . ."

" I shall myself protect this lady's honour," interposed the King loftily.

It seemed to me that the protection was like to be that afforded by the wolf to the lamb. Still, however, bad as he might be, he did not equal Jeffreys in baseness. There was something apparently in being a king.

" And I think you go too far, Jeffreys," His Majesty ran on.

" Why, you wanted to see for yourself," the other muttered.

" Will you be silent, sir? " cried the King, now thoroughly aroused and indignant at being thus shamed before the rest, at which Jeffreys slunk back, abashed.

"Your story, madam," continued the monarch, addressing me, "seemed so incredible to me that I wished to see for my own eyes what appearance you made, and by our Lady, what hath been disclosed of your temper makes me the more inclined to credit it. We have deliberated carefully with the Lord Bishop as to your future punishment, and . . ."

He stopped.

"Wouldst like to stay at our court and win our royal favour?" he asked, with a certain eager solicitation in his bearing.

At this Jeffreys' lip curled, and the Bishop looked gravely anxious. They both knew very well what he meant and so, in sooth, did I.

"Your Majesty," said I, "I must share the fortunes of my father, and I take it that his presence will not be acceptable at your court."

"Very well then," said the King, looking very much disappointed at my refusal to his sudden proposition, "we will say no more on't, save to add this, should your inclinations ever change, you will find a warm welcome here . . . I mean at court."

"I thank Your Majesty," said I.

The King turned to the Bishop, who arose,

bowed, and presented three sealed documents. The King took them in his hand and then extended them to me.

" Here," said he, " is the pardon of your father, that of Sir Hugh Richmond, and . . ." he paused as he lifted the third paper, " and your own sentence."

" And may I ask what that is, Sire? "

" You may ask," was the answer, " but you are not to be told what it is until you reach Edinburgh."

" Whatever it may be," said I, " I shall submit to it gladly in view of Your Majesty's clemency to those I came hither to save."

The King laughed uproariously.

" Don't be too sure of that," he said. " Now, Feversham, will you have this lady and these documents delivered to General Ramesay and Sir Alexander Forfair at Edinburgh on pain of our displeasure and without delay? "

" Your Majesty," I cried, " let me take the pardons there alone. I give you my word of honour, Sire, that I will not break the seal or look within that which concerns me personally, but I will deliver it as it stands, and the others also, to the Lord Chief Justice."

" Your word of honour as a man? "

" As a woman, Sire."

" And why do you wish to go alone? "

" Because I can make the greater speed if I be not hampered by an escort of soldiery."

" Would you take a woman's word, Your Majesty? " growled Jeffreys.

" Not that of the women with whom you consort, my lord," said the King caustically, " but of this one, yes.   How if you should be stopped, madam? "

" I can defend myself," I answered, " and these papers would be of no value to any one but myself. There is not a highwayman in Scotland who would despoil me of them, or who, knowing my story, would not aid my progress."

" You shall go as you came, alone," said the King.   " Feversham, take orders for the lady's departure on the morrow, escort her safely beyond the limits of the town."

" It shall be done, Your Majesty," returned the soldier.

" And now, Sire," I asked, " have I leave to retire? "

" You may go," said the King magniloquently, " and hereafter, when men speak ill of me as they often do of kings, remember that in your case at least I used you well."

"I shall not forget, Your Majesty," said I, bowing low, "your royal kindness, nor the reasons therefor," I could not help adding in spite of the danger, as I thought how I had bribed him.

The King looked at me suspiciously at this equivocal compliment, which was a great act of folly on my part, for I had not yet got away with my precious documents, but by great good-fortune for me he said nothing.

"Have I Your Majesty's leave to speak a word of farewell and acknowledgment to Your Majesty's friends?" I asked further.

The King nodded gravely.

"As for you, sir," then said I, turning to the Bishop, "you have been a father in God indeed to the afflicted and the troubled, the cast down and the weak. I shall remember it in far Scotland, and before I go, may I ask your prayers and your blessing?"

I humbly knelt before him as I had not knelt since I had knelt to the King himself when I first entered the room.

The old man, his homely face lighted with divine

and tender compassion, laid his hands upon my head and prayed for my defence.

"You have said well," commented the King, somewhat touched by this tender action, "for you owe more to the cleric than you dream of. Now, 'tis your turn, Jeffreys."

He laughed viciously.

"As for you, sir," said I, rising and turning toward him,—I stood this time with my head up and my hand upon my sword,—"I would to God I were in truth instead of seeming a man, for, saving the royal presence, I would drive this weapon through your black heart, and were there any men of my race alive, they would never rest until they had struck you down."

"Treason, treason!" bellowed Jeffreys. "She would raise a weapon against the King, his Justice, Your Majesty!"

"You brought it on yourself," said the King coolly. "Faith, I like the woman's spirit. Look to it, Jeffreys! Look to it! Hast any word for me, madam?"

"No more than I have said, Sire, save to wish that I had another five thousand pounds."

The King started.

"For Your Majesty's charities."

" You have said words enough," returned James, who evidently liked ill the turn of the conversation. "Had best withdraw from our presence now."

I went out of the chamber with my colours flying, General Feversham in attendance upon me. The gallant soldier chuckled mightily when we were safely out of earshot of the King.

" Faith, madam," he said, " you made a fine end. Ride you to-morrow morning? "

" Sir," said I, " a word in your ear. You will not betray me? "

" On the faith of a soldier, no."

" I fear the King, I fear Lord Jeffreys more. He is capable of apprehending me and destroying the pardons. Therefore, I ride to-night."

" But you are road-weary."

" What of that? I will take an unfrequented road, and lie to-morrow in some quiet spot until I be recovered."

" You shall not go alone," said Feversham. " The peril that you mention is not imaginary. I myself will ride the night through with you. Nay, I have a wife and daughters older than yourself. You may trust me without fear."

" Indeed, I do," I cried, gladly extending my

hand, which the brave soldier took and shook vigorously.

" I will see you safely over the frontiers. Damn that Jeffreys for a black-hearted villain. He is a man of peace, but he hath slain and tortured more in his Bloody Assize than even that most ruthless soldier Kirke himself."

Which was putting it pretty strongly, indeed, I thought!

Chapter
XI

Wherein Sir Hugh Richmond finds me, not unwilling, thrust upon him

SIX days after, my return progress being slower than my dash southward, I rode through the gates of Edinburgh.

The Earl of Feversham had been as good as his word. He had convoyed me by retired roads until all possibility of interference had been avoided. At the first convenient opportunity I had lain down and slept a day and a night straight through. Had I not enjoyed this chance for rest, I should have died of sheer fatigue and nervous strain. As it was, I was still a wreck of a woman when I was halted by the soldiers of the guard at the familiar city gate.

" Is your name Carthew? " cried the officer, who had been summoned by the sentry as I approached.

" Well, sir, I have sometimes been so called," I answered.

" Humph! "

He read from a lengthy written description in his hand:

" ' Young, slight, fair of face, a woman in man's attire, a riding suit of blue and silver, sometimes known as Carthew.' "

The description certainly fitted me.

" Madam, or sir, whatever you be, you are under arrest," he said. " We have been searching for you for ten days. I have orders to convey you instantly you are apprehended to the castle and turn you over to the Commandant or the Lord Chief Justice."

" I would fain make some change in my apparel, sir. You have guessed right; I am a woman. I should like to resume the garments of my sex, but after that, I shall be at your service. Indeed, you could do me no greater kindness than to take me speedily where you mention."

" I should like to oblige you, madam," said the officer, " but my orders admit of no discretion. As you are, you must be delivered to the Commandant at once."

" Very well, then. I will give you my word," said I, " if you will allow me to ride quietly by your side, to make no effort to escape your custody."

" Your word! " said the officer. " The word of one Carthew, a traitor? "

" The word of Lady Katharine Clanranald, daughter of the Earl of Clanranald, carrying messages from His Majesty, the King, to Governor Ramesay and Lord Chief Justice Forfair," I answered quite calmly.

The officer stared.

" So that's the solution of the mystery," he exclaimed. " Very well, madam, I accept your word. If you will wait here a moment until my horse is saddled, we will proceed."

His trust in my honour touched me. In a short time, his horse was brought around. He spoke to a squad of cavalry, and I riding by his side, we cantered through the streets and up toward the castle.

General Ramesay and Sir Alexander Forfair were closeted together. So soon as the officer declared who was the prisoner he brought, I was instantly admitted. It was the same chamber, I afterwards learned, in which Sir Hugh had submitted to the questioning. The two gentlemen were alone. The officer was dismissed. I was courteously invited to a seat and the questioning began.

" You are, I take it," said Sir Alexander, " Lady Katharine Clanranald? "

" I am, sir."

" You stopped the King's messenger on the King's Highway a fortnight ago? "

" I did, sir."

" You robbed him of the royal warrant for the execution of your father. This warrant was destroyed."

" I cannot deny it."

" Afterward by cajolery, or bribery, or whatever female arts or influence you possess, you suborned an honest soldier, you won him away from his duty, you made him a traitor to his King, and faithless to his cause."

" Sir," said I, " if to be touched by the misfortunes of a daughter who risked life and reputation to save her father, especially when the warrant had been destroyed before he reached me; and if to extend compassion to a woman wounded, helpless, and at his mercy be to fail in his duty, to betray his trust, to be a traitor to his King, then I suppose that I cannot deny the charge against Sir Hugh."

" Do you deny, madam," asked the Chief Justice sternly, " that it was all arranged between

you; that the scheme was concocted in the inn,
that you and he connived together by superficial
wounds, perhaps self-inflicted, to give your own
interpretation to the facts?"

Oh, how fierce was his look at poor me!

" On my solemn word, sir, as my father's daughter, I do deny that. I did deliberately rob Sir
Hugh Richmond, but without his knowledge be-
forehand. We had met in friendly converse the
night before and had conceived a mutual regard
for each other."

General Ramesay smiled, and even a flicker of
humour appeared on the face of Sir Alexander.
I resented it hotly.

" As one man and another," I cried, " for Sir
Hugh knew not that I was a woman until later.
I will admit that he was unsuspicious of me, and
that gave me the only advantage by which I could
have hoped to overcome so tried a soldier. As
for the rest, sirs, it happened as I have said. It
was pure kindness of heart toward me. And what
would have been gained by handing poor me over
to punishment since the warrant had been destroyed, sirs?"

" That was not a matter about which a soldier
need have inquired," said General Ramesay. " He

had a certain duty to do. He failed to do it. He has been arrested, tried, condemned."

" But not executed! " I cried, laying my hand upon my heart and turning very white.

" Not yet, madam," said the General, looking very stern.

" How could he be tried without me as the principal witness? "

" He hath admitted everything, except to disclose your name, rank, and whereabouts."

" Indeed, madam, you yourself are a prisoner and must submit to the same trial," interrupted the Justice.

" Nay, not so, your lordship," I answered triumphantly.

I drew from the pocket of my coat the three papers.

" Here," said I, extending one, " is His Majesty's free pardon for the Earl, my father. This," I continued, laying the other upon the table, " is a document of similar purport for Sir Hugh Richmond."

I held back the third, while Sir Alexander Forfair eagerly picked up the other two. He broke the seals, scanned them hastily, passed them to General Ramesay, and then addressed me.

" Madam, it is as you say. Never did I receive orders with a better grace, never shall I carry out royal mandates with a lighter heart. Hey, Ramesay ? "

" As for the Earl," said the General, " he is a political prisoner with whom I am not greatly concerned, but I am rejoiced indeed that my old friend and comrade, Sir Hugh Richmond, is to go free. He hath failed in his duty, 'tis true, but, by Heaven, madam, when I look at you, I find excuse for him."

" But yourself, Lady Katharine," said the Justice gravely, " you at least are not relieved by these documents."

" Sir," said I, " I have here still a third paper of importance."

" What saith it ? "

" With its contents I am not acquainted, but His Majesty did declare that it prescribed my punishment. I gave my word to him that I would deliver it to your lordship unopened, and you can testify that I do so."

" Hast not thy share of the curiosity of woman, madam ? " queried the Justice.

" Not in this case, my lord," said I boldly. " I left it with my petticoats."

"Wouldst know thy fate, girl?" he continued, breaking the seal and looking at me before he examined the contents.

"So long as my father and . . . friend are free, what happens to me is of little consequence," was my answer.

The Lord Chief Justice looked at the paper. His lips twitched. He passed it over to General Ramesay. Less controlled than the other, the soldier burst into a loud laugh.

"A sentence, indeed!" he cried. "How think you it will be liked?"

"Prisoners, I believe," returned the Justice, "are not consulted as to their likes and dislikes when sentence is passed upon them."

This was all very mystifying to me, but at least it was evident that my punishment was not very terrible. Sir Alexander and the General consulted together in whispers for a few moments, and then the soldier spoke to me.

"Madam, your sentence contemplates a life imprisonment, but under conditions which perhaps may make it bearable. I regret extremely to be compelled to communicate such unpleasant tidings to you, but I have no option, and as the sentence is to commence immediately on your arrival here,

I shall have to order you into close confinement at once."

" May I not see my father? " said I, bravely striving to keep up heart under this tremendous and surprising prospect. Indeed, I could see nothing in it to cause such laughter on the part of the two old men before me.

" Presently, madam, but not now."

" And if I might see Sir Hugh Richmond for a moment, I should like to tell him," I faltered, " that I have succeeded in securing his freedom, as I am responsible for his detention."

" Presently, presently," said the Justice. " Meanwhile, I will prepare orders for your father's freedom and for Sir Hugh's as well, but you will have to obey General Ramesay's orders. There is no choice."

" Let me see my father, then, as soon as possible, and Sir Hugh Richmond, if he care to visit me and it is permitted," said I, rising and preparing to follow the Governor.

He escorted me gravely along several corridors and down several flights of stairs until we came to the strong rooms of the castle. Summoning a turnkey, we paused before a locked and grated door.

"Your present place of detention will be here, madam," he said as the door was unlocked.

I entered the room. It was bare and simply furnished, empty of other person than myself. Some grated windows admitted light, but were so high placed that I could not see anything but sky out of them. It was indeed a prison. There was an opening in the wall beyond, closed with a door.

"Should you care to do so," said the commandant very softly, "you may open the door and enter the other room. Is there anything I can do for you before I go?"

"Send me some clothes suitable to my sex and station, if you will. Master Dunner, the advocate, will procure them, I am sure. And that is all, sir."

"They shall be sent for immediately," said the General, bowing himself out.

I heard the door close; I heard the key turn in the lock. I was alone. My great adventure was over; my punishment had begun. Well, I had saved my father's life and Sir Hugh Richmond's life. I was willing to pay the price by the long confinement to which I must perforce look forward. This was the mercy of the King! I tried to keep up a brave heart, and yet after a while I failed. I sank down on a rude chair by a ruder table, and laid my head on my arms, and cried just like any other woman.

A noise called me to myself. Fearful, I raised my head. The door to the right into the other room was open. A man stood in fair view under the arch of it. It was Sir Hugh Richmond.

" My God! " he exclaimed. " Lady Katharine, is it you? What do you here? "

" I am a prisoner," I faltered, " a prisoner for life." He came closer to me. " But you are free, sir."

" What mean you? "

" I rode south to King James. His Majesty hath been graciously pleased to pardon you,"—was there indication of my feelings in the fact that I put Sir Hugh first?—" you and my father," I said. " But me he hath condemned to imprisonment for life."

" The dog! " cried the soldier. " I renounce his allegiance. The cruel, brutal tyrant! And I have fought for him. Madam, I will not have it so. I will go to him myself and wrest from him your pardon."

" You cannot," I cried; " by the terms of your release, if you are found in Scotland within four

days thereafter, you are to be killed as an outlaw
without recourse."

"And if I were to be shot the next moment, I
would still force my way into his presence if for
naught but to tell him what I thought of him.
What is life, what is freedom for me without you?
I might not tell you before when I had rendered
you some slight service, but now when there is much
to do for you, I can declare that I love you, and
you only, and that without you life, liberty are
nothing."

"Is this," said I, "one of those protestations
which spring fortnightly from your lips?"

"Madam, it springs eternally from my heart.
I am ashamed of my foolish words."

"And your ideal woman?" I persisted.

"Lady Katharine," said the man, "I never
thought to see her, to look upon her as I do now.
I never thought . . ."

He came closer to me; he caught me in his
arms. Was I too tired or disinclined to struggle,
I wonder? At any rate, he was not to be denied
in his purpose.

"I never thought," he went on, "thus to hold
her in my arms. I never expected thus to kiss
her lips."

He suited his action to his words. And I—
what was the matter with me?—I resisted not; I
lay there trembling, thrilling—his own!

"I am a prisoner," I said at last when he gave
me breath and space to talk, although still he held
me close, and still my arms clung about his neck.
"I can be nothing to you except. . . ."

"I would tear down the castle stone by stone,
hurl the King from his throne itself, but I would
have you now," said my soldier.

Neither of us had noticed that the door at the
back of the room had opened. It was Sir Alexander Forfair's dry and caustic voice which broke
upon our passion.

"Still talking treason, Sir Hugh?" he said,
shaking his finger. "But we will overlook it this
time. We have not heard a word. Hey, General Ramesay?"

"I am as deaf as the walls, your lordship,"
replied the soldier.

Sir Hugh and I parted in great confusion. At
that moment my eye fell upon the tall figure of my
father, white-haired, bent and broken from his
long confinement. In a moment I was in his arms,
the others standing aside respectfully to let us
come together. As I hung upon my father, as he

kissed me, fondled me, and blessed me, it was Sir
Hugh's voice which interrupted us.

"Sir," said he to General Ramesay, "is that the
Earl of Clanranald?"

"The same," said the General.

"By your leave, sir," continued the young
soldier stepping forward, "I am Sir Hugh Richmond of Surrey, until recently an officer in the
King's Guards, now a disgraced soldier, and if I
understand your daughter aright, sentenced to
exile like yourself. I am not without friends upon
the continent, especially in Holland whither I propose to retire, and whither I should be glad, if your
plans permit, to have you accompany me. Nor
am I absolutely penniless, for I have certain moneys
at interest in that country which are at your service.
For the rest, I love your daughter; I would fain
make her my wife. May I have your consent to
our union, my lord?"

At this Sir Alexander and the General looked at
each other and smiled again.

"I know naught of you, sir," replied the old
Earl courteously. "You seem a gallant gentleman." He hesitated. "I am old, friendless, alone.
This is the last of my ancient race. What saith my
daughter?"

Thus adjured I spoke up bravely.

"If it pleases you, sir, to give your consent, I shall be very happy," I answered. "Had it not been for Sir Hugh's kindness to me, I had not succeeded in procuring your freedom. You know the story?"

"Master Dunner hath told me. And you wish to marry this gentleman?"

"'Tis the dearest wish of my heart," I said with growing courage and resolution.

"It is also evidently," interposed Sir Alexander Forfair, "the dearest wish of His Majesty the King's heart as well."

He lifted a paper as he spoke, which I immediately recognised.

"My punishment!" I exclaimed in amazement.

"'Tis indeed a heavy one."

"Imprisonment for life," I broke out.

"Even so, madam, but in the custody of Sir Hugh Richmond, who will give bond, a marriage bond, forthwith to safeguard the prisoner."

"With all I have, or hope to have," answered the delighted soldier.

And this time before them all once more he took me in his arms.

Outside in the corridor, a priest, the chaplain of the garrison, waited, and there before them all, clad as I was, I placed my hand in that of my soldier, and we were made man and wife.

The brief ceremony was soon over. There was little time for delay; we had but four days in which to leave Scotland, yet the others considerately withdrew, leaving me alone with my husband for a moment. The door was open and there was none to bar our going when we chose. The footfalls of my father, who was the last to go, had scarce died away in the passage when my husband took me once more in his arms.

" I feel," said I, " as if I had won you at the pistol's point."

" My lad," said he, laughing, " as I told thee before, I am glad to have thee in my company and under my command."

" You shall find me," said I, " a faithful comrade, a dutiful and obedient . . ." I paused . . . " soldier," I managed to say before he clasped me close again.

BOOK II
THE KEEPING OF A WIFE

As described by the Gentleman who did it,
with an incidental Digression by
the Lady herself

Chapter
XII

*In which I, Sir Hugh Richmond, who tell this Tale,
find that it is easier to marry Lady Katharine
Clanranald than to keep her for my own*

BEING a soldier and a veteran of many an
out-fall and on-fall, of frequent battle and
stubborn leaguer, I know that to get and
to keep are two entirely different operations. To
have and to hold, which go together in the phrase,
are not always associated in life, especially in a
soldier's life.

Through a series of the most romantic adventures and perils, which she herself most gallantly,
with some slight assistance from me, had overcome, I had got myself a wife; but as I stood on
the low bluff near Cockenzie that afternoon and
watched her being borne away, swiftly away from
me, by a small boat to a smart brigantine hove to
in the offing, it seemed to me that I had won her
but to lose her.

Enlarged from prison by her woman's wit and
married that very morning, I had counted myself

the happiest of men; now I was the most miserable.   Exiled by the King, my estates confiscate,
broke in rank—these I couid have borne.   But to
find my wife torn from me by force of arms, myself regarded with sudden hatred and suspicion
by those by whom I was surrounded, surely I
might have been forgiven if I had fallen into utter
despair.

But I was a soldier, I had bided the shock in
many a stricken field, and I knew that the battle
was not lost or won whiles I, or the enemy, could
keep that field.   Therefore I did not despair; on
the contrary, I was white hot with growing rage.

The Majesty of England was a large thing.
I was but a poor soldier, an outlaw and an exile,
a proscribed man, a death sentence hanging over
my head if I were found within the confines of the
three kingdoms within four days.   So far so good,
no worse sentence could be passed upon me.   If I
failed, I would liefer die than not without Lady
Katharine Clanranald—this morning by the grace
of God become Lady Katharine Richmond, and
my wife.   Losing her, I did not care what happened to me.

I was a tried and veteran soldier, a seasoned
man of the world, yet the passion that I had so

suddenly developed for this splendid woman might
have amazed even me, had I been capable of con-
sidering it from any point of detachment. I had
met with many women in my life, some good and
some bad,—the latter, I am afraid, predominating;
and I had been drawn in touch with all classes from
the peasant to the great dame of the court, but
I had never seen anybody who united in her own
proper person so many, or I believe I may say all,
of the qualities I loved in woman as Katharine
Clanranald. Not only her beauty, which was in-
comparable and unsurpassable, but her wit, her
bravery, her address, her—but the reader who has
read her story, even though she so modestly told it
herself, knoweth all this as well as I. Do you
wonder that I felt reckless, friend, who read this
rougher and blunter chronicle of mine, or that I
came to instant and desperate resolution there on
the shore?

The King basely, treacherously, but perhaps as
monarchs went in those days, not unroyally, had
taken my wife; I would take her back, I swore. I
would pluck that coward fox from his very throne
and, if I found a hair of her head had been in-
jured, his life should pay for it, if I were to be
hung, drawn, and quartered the next moment. I

took a solemn oath to it by the Living God, as I stood there on the bluff.

It all happened this way. We were married in the morning, there was naught to keep us in Scotland, where Master Dunner—a gentleman, truly, even if an advocate—with Master Abadie's assistance, to whom I was much indebted, foreseeing the turn of affairs, had everything in readiness, every resource that the Earl could reasonably come at instantly available.

The quicker we escaped from the reach of so uncertain a monarch as James II., the better. All men knew him well enough, but I knew him best of all, for I had served long in his Guards, so we planned instant departure.

By good fortune we found a stout ship was sailing from Cockenzie for the Low Countries that very night. It was necessary to ride thither to take passage upon her. Master Dunner cast his fortunes in with those of his patron and kinsman, the Earl, and had elected to go with us. As we were proscribed people and found not many clamouring for service with us, we chose to go as we were, without servants or further tendance than what we ourselves could easily furnish each to the other.

My wife laughingly pointed out that I could appropriately play lady's-maid to her since she had played soldier laddie to me, and though my blunt fingers were better fitted to pistol butt and sword grip, I had no doubt that I could pass a lashing for her stays or join together a hook and eye, if main strength and determination and good will were necessary qualifications.

You have seen my lady dressed as a boy before, and you might have seen her wearing her brother's clothes again that day for better convenience in riding and travelling. I do not know whether I like her better in her proper woman's gear or in men's—to tell the truth she is adorable in either —but I had such sweet associations with the latter, she was more comrade and not less wife as she bestrode her horse gallantly booted and spurred and cantered by my side, that I was more than satisfied with her election. Never hoped I to find both comrade and wife in one woman.

I doubt not I behaved like a foolish boy. Anon I trolled out a stave of soldier song. In the lonesomer parts of the road I clapped her on the shoulder when I had a chance, as if she had been a boy; yet I recognised such colour as no boy ever sported come and go in her cheek under my touch as I drew her to me and kissed her as no boy was ever kissed.

I vow, if it had given her pleasure, I would have got down in the road and let her ride over me. She bewitched me, she possessed me, she does still for that matter, I am more fond and foolish now than ever. I can master with ease my turbulent regiment of soldiers of fortune with which we were getting ready for a great adventure toward England under Dutch William, but in truth she wound me around her finger then and ever.

Did the men of my command but know it I should have been disgraced forever, and it is only of her charity that she confines her sweet dominance over me to our lodgings, in the quiet of our chamber rather than in camp and court and field. I grow garrulous as an old woman when I think of her.

Now I know full well that a soldier should ever be on the alert, but I was as unsuspicious on that mid-day as any man that lived. Monmouth's rebellion had been stamped out with such thoroughgoing ferocity by that brute Jeffreys, that there was not even a whisper of disappointment heard; not one, not even among Scotsmen. Nor were there any gentlemen of the highway to be feared, and if there were we were all armed, and Katharine was as good as a fourth man.

We rode carelessly therefore, she and I in the advance, sometimes galloping ahead until screened behind a turn of the road or a clump of trees for an exchange of kisses unseen by the Earl and Master Dunner who jogged on behind sedately. We were approaching the outskirts of Cockenzie village when the road suddenly swerved around a thick woodland toward the bluff overlooking the sea, where I marked a small brigantine in the offing and pointed it out idly enough to my Lady Katharine.

" Will that be our ship, Hugh?" asked my wife, following my hand with her eyes.

" No, Kate, I think not," I replied after a careless glance. " 'Tis too small a boat for such happiness as is ours, Sweet."

I had scarcely said the word when from out the wood which we were nearly approaching—the road running along the very verge of the low bluff that lifted it above the high tide—burst a score or more of men on foot. They were led by a person richly dressed whose features were covered with a black visard.

I had barely time to whisk out my sword

and they were on us. One fellow bolder than the rest I had spitted with the blade, but it was jerked out of my hands. The next moment I was confronted by half a dozen heavy pistols, and the leader, he of the mask, cried:

"Yield you, Sir Hugh. A motion and we blow you from the saddle."

I might not have hesitated to take the risk, although it would have probably ended in my sudden death, had I not observed that the others of my party were alike menaced. I had fronted cold steel and had looked into the open mouth of musket and pistol, ay and of cannon, too, many times, but it gave me a thrill of horror to see my wife so threatened. I did not realise that she stood in no danger, or I might have acted differently. I made up my mind quickly, as a soldier needs must, and I said with a coolness I did not feel—on account of my dear wife:

"Your arguments are too strong for me, gentlemen. I suppose you have come for plunder; my purse is in my pocket, you'll find there is little enough in it, we are exiles proscribed by King James, and . . ."

"I don't want your purse, Sir Hugh Richmond," interposed the spokesman, drawing nearer to me.

He stopped close by my side, and by a sudden impulse, for which I have ever been glad, before he could prevent it I reached over and twitched from his face with one quick movement of my hand the black mask that hid it. I recognised the man instantly.

" Stenwold! " I cried. " What does this mean ? "

He was furiously angry at being discovered and showed it now.

" By Heaven! " he roared, " I could have you shot for that."

" And since when," I sneered, " has Lord Stenwold addressed himself to the cut-purse trade upon the King's Highway ? "

Now I knew in an instant that my aggravating accusation was a false one; as in a flash I had divined the whole situation. Lord Stenwold was King James' most intimate friend, a man who would stop at nothing, honourable or dishonourable, to further His Majesty's desires. And I knew that King James, probably aided and abetted thereto by that arch-devil Jeffreys' counsel, had repented him of his clemency and that he wanted to gain possession of my wife, for what purpose I could well imagine.

I went white hot with wrath as these thoughts rushed over me. For a moment I had the baresark impulse to throw myself upon Stenwold and his gang and die fighting, and it was hard for me to restrain that impulse; yet it would have been madness, suicide, and it would have served no purpose, for it would have thrown Lady Katharine defenceless and without resource into the hands of the enemy. So, although my blood boiled in my veins, I retained an impassive front. Stenwold laughed mockingly.

"You play the game well," he said meaningly, "I didn't know you were so good an actor. I was charged to keep our agreement a secret from the lady here, but I see no need of it now. The King loyally and royally does as he said, here is your thousand pounds in gold." He laid a bulky purse across my saddle bow. "We take the lady, you the money, the King's pardon covers you for three days more, but if you be found in his realm thereafter God help you."

"Hugh," cried my wife, "what does this mean?"

"Hoity-toity," ran on that devil Stenwold, "my lady, you know very well what it means: it was all arranged between King James and yourself before you left Durham; I had His Majesty's word for it."

" Liar!" cried Lady Katharine viciously.

She was free enough of speech when the situation warranted it.

" You dog!" cried the Earl of Clanranald, leaning forward. " Do you mean to imply that my daughter——"

" The King's word——"

" Out upon the King's word. I wish to God, Monmouth——"

" Have a care, Lord Clanranald," interposed Stenwold darkly. " Your pardon I take it covers acts of the past, there is nothing to prevent me from re-arresting you and laying charges of high treason against you once more for abusing His Majesty's clemency."

" Damn his clemency and His Majesty too," roared the Earl, struggling to force his horse nearer the other. " If you are a gentleman, draw sword. I am old but I will prove you lie in your own heart's blood."

" I am not here to fight duels with men old enough to be my grandfather," answered Stenwold, coolly enough.

" With me then," I burst out.

The rogue answered me jeeringly again. He had the whip hand and he knew it.

"What benefit would it be if I spitted you or you spitted me on the road here? Besides it is all part of the game, as you know."

"You lie, in your soul," I cried, for the moment wrath getting the better of me, but Stenwold only laughed again that irritating, maddening laugh. God, how I itched to get my hand on his lying throat and shake the wretched pander to death.

"We have had enough of this," he said, turning away from me indifferently. "My lady, will you come peaceably or——"

"Hugh," cried Lady Katharine, bending toward me in wild terror, "you won't let them take me away from you?"

"Why, he hath sold you," said Stenwold. "The price hangs on his saddle bow. Come, I have no time for further parley."

Now what was I to do? Before God if I had let go of myself for a single moment I would have thrown myself upon him, yet I could have effected nothing; there were only four of us and one of us a woman, and they were a score and a half. If I had killed one or a dozen of them, what re-

mained would have sufficed to carry out their purpose, and then what would be done with my wife?

In all that broad realm there was only one man
who could succour her—myself! Was I to throw
myself away uselessly and force her to shift for
herself? Nay, I must bide my time; I must contain myself for her sake. Therefore, although to
see her manhandled and ruthlessly dragged from
her horse, torn from her saddle, almost killed me,
I sat immobile on my own steed.

"Don't hurt her," said Stenwold, never looking
my way, as if I was not worth further consideration. "We must deliver her in good condition to
the King."

Katharine made a hard struggle, she was a
strong, brave woman, but what chance had she?
She looked at me appealingly, she called my name
again and again, but I made no response. Presently realising the absolute futility of it, she
stopped and stood shuddering on the road. Stenwold's bullies closed about her and forced her to
where a small boat lay concealed beneath the bluff.
Ere she descended she turned and gave me one look
in which love and contempt struggled for the pre-
dominance. I dare say that I made a sorry figure,
sitting my horse there on the strand with King

James' guineas hanging across my saddle bow, unable to hold the wife who had risked so much for me.

"Good-by, Richmond," Stenwold called out quite airily as the boat, a large one capable of taking them all in, shoved off. "Any message for the King?"

"Thank his gracious Majesty," cried I bitterly, "for his royal conduct toward me and mine, and say to him that I hope to requite him to the full for all that he hath done."

Chapter
XIII

*Wherein I set down in due Course the Resolution
to which I came, which boded ill to the King,
as I rode southward*

MY poor wife did not look at me as the
boat rapidly drew away from the shore;
she sat helpless in the stern sheets, her
face buried in her hands. I shuddered to think of
the light in which she and the rest must have regarded me then. I had personal and unequivocal
evidence of it immediately, for I found myself
tapped on the shoulder. The old Earl of Clanranald had advanced threateningly toward me.

"You English coward!" he cried. "Was it
for this you married my daughter, who risked her
life and honour for you and me? We should have
known better than to have trusted any one who
had ever been for a moment associated with James
Stewart."

"And do you believe this monstrous lie, Lord
Clanranald?"

"Believe it? Can I not see and hear? Draw,

sir, if you have a spark of courage left, or I shall run you through where you stand!"

"I cannot fight with you," I said; "you are her father."

"The more reason."

Indeed, I felt the prick of his sword at my throat. I found I had to do something or be cut down.

"Draw quickly or I will shoot you from your saddle, you villain!" cried Master Dunner, at that time interposing and presenting a huge old horse-pistol.

There was nothing left for me. In a twinkling, my blade was in my hand. It had been restored to me by one of Stenwold's men ere they departed. As it gritted against my lord's steel, something of my self-control came back to me. He had been no mean fencer in his younger days, he could have matched any man in the three kingdoms doubtless, but now he was old, he had been some time in prison and was certainly out of practice. His force and fire were soon spent, I was his master, yet he never blenched, although he knew it as soon and as well as I.

"I tremble," he said grimly, "from physical weakness, not from fear."

" That I know," I answered.

" Finish then; you have sold the daughter; spare not the father! "

" My lord," said I, as by a sudden trick of fence I twisted his sword from his hands and flung it to the ground, " you wrong me. I neither connived at the abduction of my wife, nor will I requite your quite natural suspicion with what it merits."

" Now is it in my mind," cried Master Dunner, seeing his patron's discomfiture and peril, " to pull the trigger of my pistol."

" Do it and kill me if you will, but know that to do so is to destroy the only possible hope of rescue for the woman we all love," I returned quietly, determined to have this all over without more delay and put our affairs on a proper basis immediately.

" What do you mean? " asked Master Dunner, pistol-muzzle wavering downward.

" Think for a moment. I love your daughter, Lord Clanranald; I perilled my life and honour for her. I was attainted of treason and death had been my portion for her. I have had no communication with King James, save through your daughter. Could I, could any one, have foreseen the course of events that brought me to the Tolbooth and what hath happened since? It is absurd, sir, on its face. I wonder that you do not see it."

"But Lord Stenwold?" asked Master Dunner, somewhat shaken by my reasoning.

"Stenwold is a devil," I persisted. "Did not you see that he tried to convince me that Lady Katharine had made an agreement with the King?"

"My life on her truth and honour!" cried the Earl.

"Mine, too," said I quickly. "I would believe her innocent in the face of twenty kings, backed by as many Stenwolds."

"But why did you sit so calmly by?" faltered the bewildered old man.

"What could I have done? The four of us together might have cut down or disposed of a dozen men out of the thirty; the rest would have worked their will; there would have been no one left to save her." I gritted my teeth as I spoke: "I will rescue her, or avenge her. We alone in the three kingdoms are able to help her. Do you think that I intend to sit calmly by and let her fall into the arms of the King? It was a part of the plan to discredit me in the mind of my wife, to make it easier for him to overcome her resistance."

" But you took the money."

" Certainly; why not? We shall have need of all of it and more mayhap. We'll fight the King with his own coin."

" What mean you to do? "

" When my wife is brought before the King, I mean to be there."

" But how? "

" I don't know; I shall accomplish it in some way; I saved my own life but to lay it down again for her. God help the King when he comes under my hand! "

" My lad," said the Earl, at last convinced, " I did, indeed, misjudge you. Forgive me. My hand."

" And mine too, sir," said Master Dunner, " if in truth you will honour me."

I grasped them both eagerly, saying:

" We waste time, gentlemen; we must be doing."

" What plans have you? "

" I ride south to-night; the King was at Durham; its nearest port is Sunderland. That ship

will take her there; at least, I think so. If I could
only have some assurance . . ."

At that juncture I caught sight of a figure mov-
ing in the trees; instantly my pistol was out of its
holster and levelled in that direction.

"Hands up," I cried, "or you shall be shot
down!"

"I have no fear of your weapon, sir soldier,"
came from the coppice, "but, because I can render you service, I . . ."

"Come forth," said I, as a sturdy Scotsman
stepped out upon the road and saluted me.

"Those men raided my little farm, yonder, before you came; they rudely kissed my wife by
force; they killed my chickens, milked my cows,
and destroyed my garden. Afterwards they talked
freely enough. I know the whole plan, and would
have got to you and warned you of it had they
not kept me in close ward. They are to take the
lady to King James at Sunderland, or Monkwearmouth."

"You hear, my lord!" I cried to the Earl
triumphantly.

I opened the King's purse, got out some of the
King's guineas, and passed them over to the faithful man.

" Here's for you," said I.

" That will pay for the chickens and the milk and the other things, except the kiss and the insults to my wife."

" And who took them? " I asked.

" The man in the lead."

" I shall add your score to mine, my friend, and, rest assured, he shall pay high for both. Tell your woman so."

" I'd rather assist in the paying myself, your honour," said the Scotsman. " You see, sir, I am an old soldier and have been to the wars; I can wield a heavy claymore still; my ancestors have fought alongside Lord Clanranald's; if you wish me, I will go with you."

I looked at the man thoughtfully. He was a stoutly-built knave, of medium age, with a dependable honest look out of his eyes that promised well.

" Have you a weapon? "

" I have at the farm."

" Get it, then."

" But my wife? "

" Have you any children? " I asked.

" None; we were married a few weeks since," he answered, smiling.

" Bring her along if she will come," I answered, " and make haste."

He saluted, turned, and ran back through the trees.

" Surely you are not going to encumber yourself with a woman in this desperate venture?" protested Lord Clanranald.

" First hear my plan. With some of this money you, sir, are to get a ship; buy it, charter it, steal it if necessary. You will find what you want in Leith, doubtless. You can also enlist a half-dozen sturdy Scotsmen who can be depended upon, and you will make the best speed you can to Sunderland Harbour and wait there for me. If I do not bring Lady Katharine off to you, it will be because I am a dead man."

" We shall do as you say without fail," said the Earl. " Ours is the easier part, but how will you recognise us?"

" We must arrange upon some signal," I answered, reflecting.

" I have it," said the Earl. " We'll paint upon the mainsail my device,—a bleeding heart pierced by a long sword."

" Excellent; but if it should be night?" I queried.

" Three lanterns set as a triangle—a red one at the top, the others white."

" Admirably devised."

" But the woman, gentlemen? " said Master Dunner.

" Lady Katharine might need the assistance and companionship of a female in a ship full of men; she shall go with you, and the man I will take with me.

" Would that I could go with you instead," said Lord Clanranald.

" Nay, my lord, you have not the physical strength to ride as fast or as far as I."

" My wife, your honour! " cried the man who had given us such valuable information, now coming back to the road, while following close behind him tramped a young and pretty country wench, tearful and excited.

" I am Sir Hugh Richmond," I began, inclining my head politely toward her as I spoke. I have ever believed in treating women with courtesy, whatever their rank. " My wife hath been abducted by King James; the man who insulted you has taken her to him, and I ride forward to take her from his hands and to avenge the insult that hath been put upon us. The Earl of Clanranald here is to take ship at Leith and meet us at Sunderland, where King James awaits my wife. You, dame, will go with him. What is your name, friend?"

"Macleod, sir," he answered, "and this is Alison, my wife."

"Lady Katharine's horse is yonder; he is something light for you, but he will carry you well, I have no doubt. Now let us be about our business quickly."

"I shall be off Sunderland before you come," said the Earl. "I'll follow hard on the heels of yonder vessel."

"And I shall board you with your daughter and my wife, or you will know that I am a dead man and she is past saving."

"In that event, King James shall still reckon with me," said the Earl resolutely. "Good-bye, lad, and God bless you. Mistress Alison, Master Dunner will take you up behind him. I will gallop on ahead."

"Good-bye, good friends all," I answered, saluting them.

"May God give us success!" responded the gallant old nobleman, lifting his plaided bonnet in return.

He turned away, followed presently by Master Dunner, with Mrs. Alison riding on the croup. I sat my horse a moment and stared out to sea at the little boat bearing my wife away; then I turned, clapped my hat more firmly on my head, gathered the reins more tightly, and looked at my new friend with his long sword.

" Come," said I.

" And God help that man if he falls in my hands," he said.

" And God help the King if he falls in mine," I replied, cantering off to the south.

Chapter
XIV

Wherein, by the Grace of God, our own Deter-
mination, and the Speed of our good Horses,
we reach Monkwearmouth in Time

I DO not believe that any two men ever pushed
horse-flesh to a greater extremity than did Macleod and I on that journey south. I am reputed
to be a cool man, and it would be idle to deny that,
having been rather severely tested a great many
times in the course of my life, I had earned the
reputation, especially as more than once that life
had depended on my skill with my sword or my
quickness with my pistol. Accordingly, I fancied
myself as well able to preserve my equanimity in
times of stress and strain as any man in England,
but I declare that I never was so thoroughly
aroused and excited in my life. Our horses were
in a constant lather of sweat and foam, but the
journey was just as hard on the riders as upon the
ridden.

Macleod was a grim old soldier, and he seemed
to catch some of my determination. Lady Katha-

rine's horse had been a good one, else he would have foundered long since, and he kept pace with my spirited bay, which had carried me often in the wars and whose mettle and endurance I knew by heart. It hurt me somewhat to push the horses the way we did, but I was playing for greater stakes than were to be measured by one horse's life, or many for that matter. I had to get to Sunderland before, or at least by the time, my wife arrived there by sea.

Going by land, naturally I should have outspeeded the ship easily had luck not been so cursedly against me. In the first place, it had rained, some of the roads were almost impassable, and some of the bridges were washed out. We pushed on frantically, scarcely allowing ourselves time to eat, snatching a few moments' rest here and there, more to breathe the horses than to sleep.

It was, therefore, three days and a half after our departure that we staggered into Monkwearmouth, and drew rein before the Boar's Head Inn, hard by old Saint Peter's Church. I was familiar with the village and the town of Sunderland across the river, where in all probability we should find the King. Before I was promoted to the Royal Guards, I had been in garrison at Sunderland

Castle. This knowledge would stand me in good stead. I am a man who remembers those things, and I was glad that King James had elected to meet his pander at Sunderland. Of course I run some risk of being recognised there, but it had been half a score of years since I had visited the town and I had little to fear from that chance; little or much, however, that risk of such recognition had to be run.

It was close on to noon when we reached the Inn. Requesting food and a good rub-down for our tired horses, which Macleod was to look to, and ordering dinner to be served in a private room and to be ready within an hour, I made my way to the waterside. I had carefully fixed in my mind the lines of the brigantine which had carried away my wife, and I was concerned with anxiety to see if she were in the river yet.

There were a number of ships on both sides of the river: some tied up at the wharves and quays, others anchored in mid-stream. Not one of them was the vessel for which I looked. I was most careful in my scrutiny, and I could swear that I was right. This gave me great relief and satisfaction; I was in time.

Indeed, in spite of our delay, we had pressed

on so furiously that it was most probable that
we had arrived a little ahead of them, for out at
sea I discerned several specks that might be ships,
one of them possibly the brigantine carrying my
wife. The tide, however, was beginning to ebb,
and it would be five or six o'clock at least before
they could beat up against the off-shore breeze
and anchor abreast the town.

Mightily comforted by my observations, I suddenly bethought me to make my assurance double
sure—as Master Shakespeare saith—for I re-
paired to the office of the harbour-master and demanded speech with that functionary. I was still
wearing my guardsman's uniform. I intended
to change it for a more sober and less distinctive
garment at the first opportunity, but I was glad
now that I had not yet done so, for it won me
instant respect and prompt answer from the old sea-
dog who had charge of the water-front and the
shipping. I threw prudence to the wind and questioned him freely.

"Hath Lord Stenwold and a party from Scotland arrived with a prisoner for the King? 'Tis
an affair of State which, of course, you will not
mention."

"Not yet, your honour," answered the man,

" but I expect them in with every tide; their vessel is in the offing now, I believe."

" And how long do you think it will be before they make a landing? "

" With wind and tide against them, sir," he answered, squinting seaward down the river, " 'twill be close on to seven o'clock before they are abreast the castle."

I threw him a coin—one of King James'!—for his civility, whereat he thanked me profusely, and, bidding him not to mention it to any one, I wrapped my cloak around me and walked off again. Whatever I was to do, must be done under cover of the night. I was quite capable of confronting the King in broad day, to kill him if he had wronged a hair of my wife's head, but I was there to save her rather than to avenge her, and I did not propose to run any unnecessary or foolish risks, not because of fear for my person, but because I was bent on carrying out my plan for her dear sake.

Therefore, I went calmly back to the Inn and partook heartily of a most noble repast. The landlord himself waited upon me, and when I whispered that I was on the King's business, but the matter was to be kept secret, seeing my uni-

form as confirmation, he was vastly flattered and
promised ready compliance with any duty I might
lay upon him. I assured his silence and good faith
by a covert threat that His Majesty himself would
resent any discussion of my presence among the
gossips in the village.

In the course of conversation, I learned, to my
great satisfaction, that His Majesty had that day
chosen to lie at Stenwold House instead of Sunderland Castle.

This was an ancient seat belonging to my lord
of that name, which had been graciously put to
the disposal of this Royal Majesty, while its
owner did the King's evil errand. I learned more,
too: namely, that Jeffreys, he of the Bloody Assize,
was also in Sunderland, where he had been holding his outrageous court. The landlord charac-
terised him as:

" A royal good gentleman, your honour, fond
of wine and woman and gaming; hath been here
in this very hostelry of mine three nights
a-running."

I knew something of the loose habits of the
bloody villain, which, indeed, were no secret to
any one well informed as to the doings of the
court, and so far as I had formulated any plan I

had counted upon this knowledge. For once Fortune was playing in my hands.

"Think you he will be here to-night?" I asked, disguising my eagerness by assumption of indifference.

"Ay, 'tis more than likely he will be, your honour."

"Very good," said I. "When he comes, apprise me of the fact without mentioning it to him; I would fain surprise my lord—by the King's command! His Majesty loveth a jest and we have set a pretty trap for the Lord Chief Justice. 'Tis a wager, understand?"

"Certainly, your worship," answered the landlord, rising to the question like a gudgeon to the baited hook as I slid a coin—another of the King's hoard!—carelessly over the table to him. Like all Englishmen, he was full of sporting blood and dearly loved a bet. "I understand, your excellency," he said as he pouched the guinea, which also he dearly loved. "Trust me, sir."

"Now, another favour," I continued. "My man, here, is from the north and is unfamiliar with the shops of Sunderland; would you execute a small commission for me?"

"With pleasure, your excellency."

" We have ridden hard on the King's service and have left our mails behind,"—which was true enough, by the way,—" I want a suit of apparel. Canst get it for me among the shops of thy friends in Sunderland? "

" I have a brother in the trade and all the gentry of the county buy . . ."

" Say no more," said I. " There are ten guineas,"—again more of King James'!—" get me the best you can, something quiet and unobtrusive, rather suited for out-door use than for the court, yet rich and elegant, such as a gentleman should wear. You are about of my own build, although somewhat stouter; what fits you will doubtless suffice for me."

" The amount is ample for the purpose, your excellency," said the landlord, taking the money; " indeed, much more than . . ."

" Whatever is unexpended you may keep for your trouble."

" Your excellency overwhelms me," returned the delighted man. " They shall be here within the hour. I am proud to be much of a size with your honour."

" Very good," said I, " and, mind, no talking—by order of the King."

"I shall be silence itself," returned he, turning to do my errand.

The rain of golden guineas which I had produced so generously on every occasion was having tremendous effect upon him. Only the very great or the very noble could, in his mind, thus indifferently dispose of precious treasure. It was money well spent, however, since it made him entirely submissive to my will.

"Go now, then," said I, "for I am in something of a hurry."

The landlord instantly bowed himself out, and I could hear him bustling about in the public room, bawling for his coat and hat with vast importance, while making ready to execute my commission.

"What think you, Macleod?" said I, rising from the table and bidding him take my place and fall to on the ample remains of the meal; "is the man true?"

He was a shrewd observer, this Scotsman, I had found, and I wanted his judgment on this important point.

"A good deal depends upon this landlord," I added.

"So long as you rain guineas upon him, you've

got him body and soul, your honour," he answered
drily.

"Thanks to the King," laughed I, lifting the
still rather full purse, "the fountain has not yet
run dry."

We had divided it equally between Lord Clanranald and myself ere we parted at Cockenzie,
and, though I had spent of my share freely, much
still remained.

"But it likes me ill," said Macleod covetously,
"to see such good gold lavished on such a
wastrel."

"There will be plenty for us all," said I, "can
I once win away with my wife."

"I care not how plenty they be, sir," was his
courteous answer, "a guinea's a guinea, whether
there be one or a thousand."

"Here's one for you then," said I, "since you
like them so well."

"I no meant my words for that," answered the
worthy Scotsman, "but I will e'en take the guinea
just the same."

"I am going to lie down now and get some
sleep, and I recommend you to do the same when
you have finished your meal. Leave word that I
am not to be disturbed, and, if I do not happen to

be awake at five of the clock, you are to come and rouse me."

" Very good, sir," replied my good attendant, whom I had learned to trust; " I'll first take a look at our horses and then I'll be blithe to follow your honour's advice."

I left him finishing the remains of the meal and withdrew to an inner chamber. Taking off my coat, and kicking off my riding-boots, I threw myself on the bed, and for three hours I slept as sound as ever I slept in my life. When I opened my eyes my watch told me that it was now five o'clock. I had taught myself the valuable habit of awakening whenever I wanted to when on service or in the field, and I had the practice down to a nicety. I was very much refreshed from my eating and sleeping, and, after I had given myself a fine wash in a tub that I caused to be brought to me, I felt fit for anything, even to the bearding of a king!

When I was ready for them, Macleod, who had also been asleep, brought me the clothes the landlord had procured. It was a rich suit of dark blue laced with silver, which fitted me well and seemed not unbecoming, though I do look my best in the noble scarlet of the Royal Guards, according to Kate, my wife. I put it on at once and, finding it so satisfactory, I sent out another guinea to the worthy Boniface, bidding him prepare supper for us. We sat down to it at six o'clock. I waived ceremony on this occasion, and Macleod, who modestly placed himself at the far end of the table, ate with me. We both proved good trenchermen.

I suppose it was near on to seven o'clock when we finished. I had no idea where we might get our next meal, and we were both of us old enough soldiers to appreciate the prime importance of attending well to the commissariat while we had opportunity.

It was perhaps half-past seven when we trotted away from the Inn yard, both of us wrapped in long cloaks, with our hats pulled well down over our faces and with our pistols carefully loaded and primed in our belts. I did not intend to be caught napping by the King at this time with empty weapons, as I had been by my wife before. We made our way to the river-bank, and followed the road to the landing in the direction of Stenwold House.

It was still light, and I observed a brigantine slowly beating up the river. My heart leaped at the sight of her. I would know that ship in a thousand. It was she. I raised my hand and shook it toward her as she came slowly on. Stenwold and my wife would be aboard. I was in good time, thank God!

For a moment I considered whether it would be possible to ambush the party who would bring Lady Katharine to the shore and sweep her away from them as soon as they landed. But I reluctantly abandoned that idea. We two could do little with so many as they would be. We must try strategy instead of force. I had devised a better plan.

I could not wait until the brigantine anchored, not even to catch a glimpse of my Lady Katharine as they landed. We trotted at a sharp pace back to the Inn, where the landlord gave me further interesting news: he advised me privately that Lord Jeffreys had sent a messenger there to say that he expected to pass the evening and the night at the Inn,—I had intended to summon him myself otherwise,—he was coming incognito, and a certain dame was to be notified to meet him. I laughed.

" By the King's command, I'll be the only lady that he'll see."

"It will be a royal jest," said the landlord, also greatly amused.

"His Majesty will be much pleased when he hears of it," said I.

"I hope, sir, that the King may be pleasured, indeed," said he.

"No doubt of it," I returned.

"And you will tell him, please your honour, that I did my small part to your entire satisfaction, sir?"

"I will see that your zeal is properly rewarded."

"What must I do further?" asked the delighted landlord.

"This," said I: "since his lordship is coming on an errand of love,"—I paused; the landlord nodded,—"he will require a private room in which to receive the person whom he expects to meet. Do you contrive that I shall be there in her place."

"And what then, sir?"

"Nothing then," said I, laying my finger by the side of my nose. "I shall do all the rest. My lord will require the room for the whole night and must on no account be disturbed. The lady must not be notified."

" You mean no harm to the King's Justice? Forgive the question, your excellency," said the landlord, rather anxiously.

" 'Twould be a hanging matter to meddle with him, my good friend. Rest easy; his Majesty loves his Chief Justice and would not have a hair of his head harmed. Know you my Lord Jeffreys' seal? "

" I happen to know it, for he hath despatched letters by me. I have seen it on all papers I take from him, and his signet ring as well."

" Good! This is a most secret business," said I, " and, while you would doubtless be well rewarded for your assistance, I would not answer for your head should you betray me." I softened this threat with another guinea—King James' again! " The King is a royal paymaster," I added knowingly.

" Everything, your excellency," said the landlord, now completely at my disposal, " shall be exactly as you wish it."

" And I myself," I continued, " am not without interest at the court. This night the King will deny me nothing. I am sure you seem a man to be trusted; there is a lady in the case, you comprehend? "

Of course he comprehended!

Presently I found myself in a very lofty and spacious chamber, the best in the Inn. Adjoining it was a smaller bedroom, whose one window looked upon the deep and silent close of the Cathedral, now deserted. The chamber was admirable for my purpose. In the bedroom I stationed Macleod. I had directed him to procure a quantity of light yet strong rope, and by some means, like the faithful fellow that he was, he had managed to obey my rather difficult order: he had the most of it wound about his person. There were a number of candles burning in the great apartment. I extinguished them all but one, and, drawing back so as partly to be concealed by the window, I loosened my sword in its sheath and waited for the coming of Lord Jeffreys with what patience I could muster—but little, I will admit.

Chapter
XV

Shows how the Lord Chief Justice of England kept a Love Tryst and what befell him at the Boar's Head Inn

IT seemed hours, although really but a few minutes, before there came a discreet tap upon the door. Before I had time to say a word, it opened cautiously and the burly figure of a man muffled in a long cloak entered the room. The door was closed behind him. He took off his hat, unbuttoned his coat, and dropped it carelessly in a chair.

" 'Tis so dark in here, Doll," he began, in a rough, hoarse voice, " that I couldn't see a blush on your face, even if you could conjure up one." He peered about him in the half-light uncertainly. " Why so sparing of the candles? " he asked with a coarse laugh. " Come, no tricks, you baggage; where are ye? "

He looked about him a moment more, fortunately not seeing me behind the hangings, and then strode boldly across the room and laid his hand on the bed-chamber door.

"Art couched already, wench?" he chuckled out.

As noiselessly as a cat, and with more swiftness than he had exhibited, I had followed him and, as his hand touched the door handle, I pricked him on the shoulder with the point of my sword. He wheeled around with a marvellous swiftness for a man of his bulk and confronted me. He did not yet recognise me in the dim light, but he saw enough to know that it was the tall form of a man in the room he expected to be welcomed to by a woman. He opened his mouth, but, before he could make a sound, I said:

"Unless you want me to run you through with this blade, you will be absolutely silent, sir."

I never saw a more ridiculous spectacle than he presented—his mouth open, his fat face violently flushed. Like most bullies—not all—this blood-thirsty jurist—God save the mark—was an arrant coward. He shrank back against the wall and only stopped retreating when further escape was impossible.

"Do you know what 'tis you are doing?" he growled. "You are raising sword against the

Lord Chief Justice of England; your life will be forfeited, 'tis treason. I will have you hung, drawn, quartered. Drop your blade instantly, knave," he went on, gaining courage as he heard his own voice.

" I would not hesitate to raise this blade against the King himself," answered I coolly.

" What, sirrah . . ." he began.

He was so accustomed to browbeat helpless victims who came before his court that his course was as natural as breathing, but I was not a victim and this was not a court, as he should very soon find out.

" And I am quite aware," I interrupted, " of all that I risk. It disturbs me not a whit. In faith, were I you, my lord, I would not dwell too much on what may happen to me in future; your present predicament is your chief concern. I advise you to give heed to it."

" Is it my money you want? " he asked, growing more and more alarmed.

" Nay," said I, " keep your hands by your side."

My sword made little circles about his throat. It was a trick of fence I had learned and it added greatly to his discomfiture.

"Take away that blade," he pleaded.

"When it suits me," I replied.

I edged around him until I could reach the bed-room door. I knocked upon it, and instantly Macleod presented himself. It pleased me to see that he had his old and terrible Scottish claymore bared and ready.

"Who is this?" asked Jeffreys, with a new accession of alarm.

"You will learn presently, my lord, that it is now not for you to ask questions, but to answer them."

"What would you, sir?" asked Macleod of me.

"Lights," said I. "I have no doubt that Lord Jeffreys would fain know whom he entertains; but first bolt the door into the hall."

"One shout," growled the Lord Chief Justice, "and I could arouse the Inn."

"But you would be so sound asleep, my lord, on the next second, that no shouting that I have heard would suffice to awaken you. Dost take my meaning?"

"Curse you, yes!"

"Remember, then, to speak softly till I give you leave to call."

While I had spoken, Macleod had barred the heavy door precluding any chance interruption; although I trusted to the landlord's zeal and devotion to prevent that, it was well not to neglect any precaution. Then, from the solitary candle, he lighted a number of others. My back was to the light, but presently I moved to let it shine upon my face.

"Richmond!" gasped Jeffreys, turning a shade paler under his red.

"The same, sir."

"What do you here?" queried the Lord Chief Justice. "You are a proscribed outlaw; I can order you seized and executed without formality of a trial; you have no standing in the court."

"I know that full well," said I. "I knew it before I heard it from your lips, worthy master of the law, and therefore your repetition of it affects me not at all."

"What do you want?" asked the frightened blackguard blusteringly.

"A small thing, an it please you—my wife."

"You fool," he muttered under his breath, "I haven't got her. Go to the King."

"That I shall, sir."

The incautious admission of the Lord Chief

Justice that I should seek the King apprised me of what I had more than suspected, that he was in the base plot.

" I mean I know nothing of her," he began, seeking to cover his blunder.

" I am glad to find out from you where she hath been taken."

Jeffreys laughed. He saw that I knew, and that I was not to be put off. Besides, his natural viciousness would not let him lose so good an opportunity to taunt me, even at so great a risk to himself.

" The King hath some spirit, after all," he said meaningly.

" Now, by the God above us," I hissed, " I could kill you for those words."

And, but I needed him, I would have done it then and there. The world would have been well rid of so low and base a villain that disgraced the judicial ermine that he wore.

" I did but jest," he said, in cowardly confusion. " It was the King's will. I had naught to do with it."

" Don't jest that way again or I might indulge my own humour, which, I assure you, hath a more biting point than yours;" and, as that point was plainly visible to him, he could not have missed my meaning. " I know perfectly well that you and that pander Stenwold are as much responsible as the cowardly King, whom I have served long enough to estimate at his true worth, or worthlessness. He hath exiled me, he hath stolen my wife; I am no longer his man, but Prince William's, across the water, and, when we come back, God help King James and you ! "

" I am sure," protested Jeffreys, " that I wish you well and . . ."

" No more of that," I said curtly.

" I'll e'en help you to get your wife," he ran on, " if . . ."

" I intend that you shall do so without conditions."

" But I am helpless here," continued my lord. " Release me and I will go to the King . . ."

" I know a better way than that," I said.

" What way ? "

" I will bring my wife from his Majesty's hand with an order from you, my lord."

" From me ? I don't understand you. I cannot issue orders to the King, sir. You rave."

" Nay, I was never soberer. I shall tell the King that I have you in safe ward; it will be her life or your life. If a hair of her head is harmed, you shall pay."

"My God, man!"

"The King loves you, you say."

"Yes, but . . ."

"Have you no confidence in the reality of his affection?"

"Ay, surely, but . . ." he began, more feverishly.

"Enough," said I. "I have decided, and from my decision there is no appeal to any court. On yonder table are writing materials; go to it; write as I dictate."

"Nay, good Sir Hugh, I . . ."

"Hesitate but a moment and I will make your life pay before I have ascertained that she has suffered. You know, Lord Jeffreys, that I have nothing to lose."

"I'll write, I'll write, but be not so hasty with thy point, Richmond."

"No more," said I. "Take the quill."

"What shall I write?" he asked, seizing the pen.

And thus I dictated to him:

"For God's love, Your Most Gracious and Royal Majesty, I am held prisoner by Sir Hugh

Richmond, who threatens me with instant death should his wife suffer any mistreatment at Your Majesty's hands. I have served you well, Sire; leave me not now defenceless in mine enemy's hand. Sir Hugh is desperate; he will kill me. I fear me for my life. Your most faithful humble servant."

He wrote it all down at my dictation.

" Hast finished? " I asked.

He nodded his head.

" Sign it."

He scrawled beneath it, " Jeffreys, Lord Chief Justice of England."

" Seal it," said I.

His hands trembled so he could scarcely drop the wax, his mouth was so dry it was difficult to moisten the seal, but he managed somehow or other.

" You never wrote truer words in your life," I said, taking the paper, and the seal as well, and examining both of them carefully, keeping him well covered the while, to see that he had played me no tricks in his writing.

" What next? " he asked.

" Go into yonder room." I pointed to the bed-chamber.

" I have done what you asked, you would not murder me now? The laws of war require that a hostage be kindly entreated and . . ."

" I intend to lock you there until I have seen the King. Go ! "

Seeing no help for it, he rose to his feet and entered the room, followed by me and Macleod. Jeffreys continued to protest, but I silenced him with that wonderfully bright persuader in my hand.

" Now that I have the letter," said I, " I care little whether you are alive or dead, and, for the toss of a coin, I would rid the world of you. But I am not a judge; being only a poor soldier, I'll keep faith with you. Your life depends entirely upon your absolute obedience; I must bind you securely."

He said no more, but suffered himself to be bound without resistance. Macleod had brought plenty of rope; we lashed him until he was as immobile as an iron bar; then we picked him up and laid him on the bed and, with what remained of the rope, secured him so that he could not move about or roll off to the floor.

" You will be enlarged, doubtless, in the morning," said I. " I wish some of Monmouth's friends and followers whom you hounded to death could see you now."

"For God's sake," he gasped, "if you must leave me this way, give me a draught of wine!"

"Nay," I replied smilingly. "Here is something that will suit your thirst and dry humour much better."

I crammed into his huge mouth, which he had opened gaspingly to protest, a soiled towel which I took from the wash-stand. I rammed it in hard and, with a piece torn from the sheet, I bound it down around his head and neck. I thought my lord's veins would burst in his forehead, he grew so purple.

"A pleasant night to you," said I. "And may the love of your King secure your release in the morning."

We extinguished the candles, went out into the large room, and closed the door. In a voice that Jeffreys within could easily hear, I said to my man:

"You will stay here on this side of the door until I send for you in the morning. If the prisoner by chance should get free of his bonds, or should fall from his bed, or should make any outcry, go in and kill him without further delay. You understand?"

"I do, sir, and it shall be as you wish," he answered loudly.

Macleod ostentatiously drew a chair up in front of the door and then, as I had need of him and could not leave him there, he rose from the chair and noiselessly followed me down the room. We extinguished the lights in the outer chamber, and, having locked all doors, took the keys with us. We had but little fear, unless some alarm was given, but that the Lord Chief Justice would be quite safe for the night, and that he was going to pass such night as he had never passed before. We waited to see the landlord, and I bestowed upon him some more of King James' his guineas. I showed him the letter sealed with Lord Jeffreys' seal. He could not read it, but he recognised the signet.

"I know that seal full well," he said, entirely satisfied by it.

"My Lord Jeffreys hath retired for the night, and upon no chance is he to be disturbed until morning, unless I should come back or send. He doth not wish the lady you know to be sent for."

"I understand," he said knowingly. He was a wise and understanding landlord indeed!

"The door is locked behind us," I added,

"and, if you value your life, keep away from it and keep others away as well."

"Your excellency shall be obeyed."

By this time Macleod and the hostler of the Inn had brought around the horses again. We mounted them once more and cantered down the street until we struck the river road. So far everything had gone without a hitch. The King lay at Stenwold House; my wife had been recently brought there. Access to him would be difficult, doubtless, but I now had means to open the gate and pass the guard. Once inside it would go hard if I did not effect Katharine's release.

If Clanranald had succeeded in his part of the plan all would be well. He ought not to be more than five hours behind the brigantine, I thought. As we got away from the houses, we eagerly searched the sea, and sure enough, between the far-away lighthouses on either side of the river-mouth, there was a vessel. It was so dark we could not have seen her had she not carried three lights set in a triangle, a red one at the top! Clan-ranald was on time. The tide now approaching full flood, he ought to be abreast Stenwold House in a few hours. We set spurs to our horses and dashed on rapidly.

Chapter
XVI

*How My Lord Stenwold settled his Account and
paid his Debt in full*

STENWOLD HOUSE stood on the bank of
the river, about half-way between Monk-
wearmouth town and the lighthouse on
the point that jutted out seaward far beyond. It
was some distance from the outskirts of the village, and I noted, as we galloped along, that the
surrounding country was lonesome and desolate.

I had at first intended to take Macleod into the
castle with me, but a better thought came to me
as we rode. Long before we reached the house
I drew rein and, to Macleod's great and over-
whelming disappointment, I outlined exactly what
I wished him to do.

" Upon second thoughts," I said, " I will not
take you with me further. Do you go back to the
village and get a boat, a wherry that two of us
can row and yet one that you can manage yourself on a pinch, and bring it to the river-bank
under the walls of the castle yonder."

"But Lord Stenwold, sir," protested the worthy Scotsman, who evidently would fain play a bolder part.

"I'll take care of him," I replied.

"I would like it well," persisted my attendant stoutly, "if I could take the payment for that kiss myself."

"Do not fear, man," said I, "I'll take payment for us both, and, unless I blunder strangely, he will never live to kiss another woman after this night. You could not do any special good with me in the castle. The two of us could not take the place by force, and, for strategy, one is as good as two or a thousand—ay, better. You can serve us all, and your revenge, best by providing the means of escape. I am like to need it both sorely and quickly to-night."

"Yonder's our ship, sir," he said, silenced by my emphasis.

"Yes, I have marked her."

We both stared seaward at the lights. I was sorry that I had not arranged some method of signalling the Earl, but none that I could have thought of would have been practicable and, indeed, any attempt at it would infallibly have betrayed us.

"Am I to rent, borrow, or steal a boat, your honour?" asked Macleod, appreciating the fact that my decision, which was only common-sense, was unalterable.

"You are to be here within the hour with the boat. I care not how you get it. That's your own lookout, but get it. Don't fail me; remember your wife is on that ship; and it might be convenient for you to bear in mind that Lord Jeffreys has had ample opportunity to familiarise himself with your face and figure as well as with mine, and I would not give a penny for your life if you are in England when he gets loose."

"I shall be there within an hour," answered the Scotsman stoutly. "This horse, sir?"

"You can't take him aboard ship," I replied; "you must leave him behind."

"Very good, sir." He half-wheeled his horse and then stopped. "You are going on a desperate venture for your wife," said he; "if a poor man might be so bold . . ."

His hand went out toward me rather tentatively in the darkness. I waived the difference in rank at once—for that matter, I have ever been willing to shake hands with honest men, even those of low degree.

"Good luck and God bless you, sir," he said
earnestly.

"Thank you," said I. "Don't fail me," I repeated again.

"I will meet your honour in an hour, yonder,"
he replied.

With that he put spurs to his horse and galloped away. Now what was I to do? It was evident that it might be difficult to get entrance to
Stenwold House, and more difficult to get access
to the King. I did not want to play my trump
card, Lord Jeffreys' note, until the last moment.
Yet, what could I do without it?

If I had time, I might perhaps have managed
to scale the walls in some way and effect an entrance by stealth, but I had no time. Too much
had been wasted as it was. I judged it to be about
eight o'clock. I was morally certain that I would
be in good time, but I did not dare to tempt Fortune too long and too much.

I knew that King James would at first try
cajolery and persuasion—that was his usual
method; not until they failed would he try bribery, being a niggardly monarch, and only in the
last instance would he resort to force. I could
picture accurately what was about to happen, the

course of affairs was clear to me, but to effect anything I must get in the castle, and boldness was my only resource.

It was fortunate for me that the King had chosen to lie at Stenwold House instead of the Castle at Sunderland, across the river. It would have been difficult, if not impossible, to have effected my purpose had he been there. Here it was easier. At most he would be surrounded by but few of his guards; perhaps he would be depending entirely upon Stenwold's retainers for protection. The King was not more bold in his debaucheries and abductions than he was on the field of battle or anywhere else, and it may be that some lingering sense of shame might cause him to conduct his disgraceful amour in secret when he could do it.

I did not stand still in the road making these reflections; on the contrary, they came to me as I galloped swiftly toward the house.

The castle was an old one, built God knows how many centuries before and added to from time to time. The rambling walls were surrounded by a moat now gone dry, which was crossed by a drawbridge never raised. I thundered up to the gate at full speed, flung myself from my horse, knowing full well he was tired and would stand until doomsday, unless driven away, in case I needed him again. And, with the hilt of my sword, I knocked heavily upon the panel of the great door.

A wicket-gate at the side was instantly opened and a man in the uniform of the King's Guards peered through. Light was shed upon us from a flaming cresset hanging over the arch of the main door; by it I saw him plainly and recognised him, too. His name was Harkins; he was a sergeant, an old comrade and friend who had been in my own company of the Royal Guards. The recognition was mutual, but, before he could speak, I interrupted him.

"Sergeant," said I, "you don't know me, you have never seen me before, understand?"

"N-n-no, sir," was the astonished answer.

"Well, these are facts; get them in your mind," I insisted sharply.

"Very good, sir," he answered slowly, beginning to comprehend, "I don't know your honour, I have never seen you before."

"That's it; you will be glad you did not recognise me to-morrow."

The sergeant nodded, he was not a stupid man.

and he began to see the reason for my strange course.

"And now," said I, "I am a messenger from my Lord Chief Justice, a private messenger, who must see the King instantly. Lord Jeffreys is now at the point of death, his life's in the greatest danger."

"But, your honour," stammered the sergeant, "it will be impossible to see the King to-night. He's got a woman with him, and Lord Stenwold himself keeps everybody from him."

"That woman is my wife," said I grimly.

"Good God, sir!" exclaimed the sergeant. "What do you want me to do?"

"First of all, admit me; then take me to the Officer of the Guard—who is he? Do I know him?"

"No, sir, it is Leftenant Brayford; he's a new officer, your honour, and he is at play with Ensign Scarlett in his quarters off the guard-room. They are drinking too, sir."

"Good," said I. "That leaves you in virtual command of the guard?"

"It does."

"Go to Mr. Brayford, and tell him that an urgent messenger from Lord Chief Justice

Jeffreys desires to see Lord Stenwold on a most serious business, and contrive that you shall be the one to conduct me to him."

" I think that will be easy, sir," said the sergeant, closing the wicket and marching off.

It was fortunate that I had found old Harkins at the gate; the man had been devoted to me and was as faithful as the day was long. Whether his devotion to me would overcome his duty to the King was a thing I could not decide, and I stood there, leaning against the rough stones of the wall, a prey to the intensest agonies of apprehension I had ever experienced, lest I should be denied entrance and stopped helplessly at the very beginning of the undertaking on which so much depended. My relief was correspondingly great when the door opened and honest old Harkins appeared again.

" I am to conduct you to Lord Stenwold, by orders from Leftenant Brayford, who, with Mr. Scarlett, is well in liquor now, sir," said the old soldier.

" This will cost young Brayford his commission, mayhap his head, I fear me," said I under my breath.

" And me mine, as well it may be, Sir Hugh," answered Harkins simply, but making no pause on that account.

"Man," said I earnestly, "I am off for the Low Countries to-night with my wife, if all goes well. There is plenty of soldiering and good pay there. We have served together for many years; come with me."

"That will I gladly if you will take me, Sir Hugh," answered Harkins earnestly, and evidently pleased.

"Good; if you serve me well in my great need this night, I promise you shall never have cause to regret it."

"What do you propose to do, sir, if I may make bold to ask?"

"To take my wife from the King, even if I have to kill him."

"Good God, sir, I hope it won't need to come to that!"

"It is not likely," said I contemptuously. "The King will give way before he dies."

"Yes, sir," answered the old man thoughtfully. "He ain't the bravest King on earth."

"No, but we waste time."

"Very good; come this way, sir."

I muffled my face in my cloak and disguised my

walk so that none of the men on guard or loung-
ing in the courtyard, waiting for their tour of
duty to begin, would by any chance recognise me.
The sergeant made his way quickly across the
courtyard and entered the main building, with me
hard at his heels. We proceeded down a large
hall, up a long flight of steps, and into a vast
apartment, at the further end of which and
before a door a soldier stood guard. We marched
straight up to him.

"Is Lord Stenwold within?" asked the sergeant in a low voice as the man saluted him.

"Yes, sir," was the whispered reply, "and he
hath left strict order that no one is to disturb him
on any account."

"There is a messenger here from the Lord
Chief Justice Jeffreys," returned Harkins quickly,
"who must see the King on a matter of life and
death. He must have access to Lord Stenwold;
when I have turned him over to my lord my responsibility ceases."

"But, sergeant . . ." began the man, unwilling either to disobey Lord Stenwold's order or too
obstinately to resist his sergeant.

"Enough," said old Harkins peremptorily.
"You will take your orders from me; I will re-

lieve you at this door and guard it myself; you go to the further end of the hall, station yourself outside yonder door, and keep out anybody and everybody at every hazard till you are relieved."

" Orders are orders," said the soldier resign-edly, " but the responsibility will be yours."

" It is mine," assented Harkins.

The man shouldered his halbert and marched down to take the post designated—outside the en-trance door, through which we had come, at the far end of the hall. It had all been cleverly thought out by the sergeant. I had not given him credit for such shrewdness. Whatever happened behind that closed door that gave entrance to my Lord Stenwold's retreat would have few auditors and all but one as far away as possible. I thanked him with word and look.

" Now, your honour," said he, " it rests with you. I will keep this door as long as I can; I will give it up to no one, unless the Leftenant or the Ensign should make their rounds. I don't think that likely, but the guards will be relieved at ten and you have but a short time at your disposal."

" I do not want much time," I replied. " No matter what you hear, keep fast by the door, un-

less I call you. I'll soon be back, successful, or
I'll be dead, in which case remember you do not
know me."

" Very good, sir, and God help us all."

" Amen," said I.

The hurried conversation had been carried on
in low whispers, so as to give no possible alarm.
I laid my hand upon the door. Fortunately it was
unlocked, and gave under my gentle pressure.
What had Stenwold to fear, and why should he
lock himself in? All the doors in Stenwold House
were secret and noiseless, especially those in my
lord's private apartments. This one opened
without a sound, and, with a stealthy motion that
would not attract attention, I stepped noiselessly
into the room.

This apartment was smaller than the other,
which had been possibly designed for a refectory
in days gone by, and was evidently a library. It
looked toward the sea. Heavy hangings draped
the windows, a thick carpet lay on the floor. The
place was richly furnished and brightly lighted
from many candles in sconces and hanging lustres
of candelabra. In the centre of the room, by
the side of a small table, reclined Lord Stenwold,
in somewhat negligent disarray, in a large and

comfortable chair. On the table were bottles and glasses and the remains of a meal. Lord Sten-wold had evidently just finished his repast. He was engaged in the pleasant act of leaning back in his chair and yawning, stretching out his hands the while. His back was toward the door and nothing had as yet apprised him of my presence. I slipped my sword out of the scabbard as gently as possible. I thought I made no sound, but evidently I did, for he was on his feet in a minute and facing me.

" Richmond! " he gasped, in a low, strained voice, evidently not caring or daring to arouse the King or the house. " Good God! "

His hand reached for his own sword, lying on a stool by his chair. I could have spitted him then and there without risk or trouble, but it was ever against my principles to attack an unarmed man, and I let him seize his weapon. I said in a voice low to match his own, but full of vengeance and hate :

" You vile pander, you have come to the end of your tether now."

Stenwold menaced me with his point and then sneered.

" Why, you fool," he exclaimed, " this is my

house! I have but to call out and the King's Guard will be on you in a moment. To-night His Majesty would be private yonder with a lady. I would not have him disturbed. Yield you at once. If the lady be in a melting mood, as I doubt not, sweet remembrances of their pleasant love passages may incline the King to clemency in the morning when you sue."

I needed nothing more, but, if I had, that last mordant insinuation would have been enough. I advanced on him with such fury, forgetful of everything, that he opened his mouth to cry out in his alarm; ere he could do it, I whipped out a small pistol of French make, which I carried ever in my pocket, and held it toward him in my left hand.

" You know," said I, " that I am a dead shot with either hand, and I swear to God that I will put a bullet through your black heart if you make a sound, if I am to be torn to pieces the next second."

" You have an advantage over me," said Stenwold coolly. He had recovered himself and seemed a little ashamed of his lapse. " I have naught but my sword."

To do him justice, the villain was brave enough,

I knew; yet, as he said, he was armed only with his sword.

"I don't intend to use the advantage," I replied, "unless you force me to it. If you will agree to stand up and fight like a man and in silence, you shall have your chance."

"Done!" said the man quickly. "My word of honour against yours, that whichever of us dies does it silently."

I laid the pistol on the table on the instant.

"There's my answer. Now, on guard!"

It was no light task I had before me. Stenwold was one of the best fencers in the King's realm; he and I had enjoyed friendly bouts many times, although I never liked him, and more often than not he had bested me, although I was counted something of a master of the white weapon myself. In a scientific engagement he was pretty certain to get the better of me, but this was *guerre à outrance,* and at that sort of a game I felt I would be his master. Neither did I intend to delay matters, nor did I desire to fill the room with noise of ringing steel.

We fell easily into position; he made the first lunge at me, as I knew he would. Contrary to the rules of fencing, I parried it with my left arm, his point grazing through the flesh between my elbow and shoulder, as I expected. Heedless of the pain, with that I closed with him to his great surprise, and, before he could disengage or divine what I would be at, I shortened my sword and drove it home, through his heart.

It was quickly done and soon over. He reeled and threw up his hands; I dropped my own blade to the carpet, which luckily prevented noise; caught him in my arms and eased him down. He was stone dead by the time I laid him on the floor.

I will admit that I felt no remorse whatever. The last taunt about my lady had maddened me. I had killed him with as little compunction as if he had been a rat, which indeed he was. Drawing his blade from my sleeve, I laid it across his breast. Resuming my own sword, I stepped to the piece of tapestry over the door which he had pointed out to me, behind which I knew I should find the King and my wife.

Chapter
XVII

In which Lady Katharine Richmond, at the Request of her Husband, tells how she and Lord Stenwold came to Stenwold House

AT the request of my dear husband, Sir Hugh Richmond, I take up the telling of this strange, yet true, tale for a little space. He did the same for me when the narration of events was in my hand, and I can do no less for him; besides, he is my true and lawful lord, and I owe him duty and I pay him love unbounded, the more especially the latter, because I so basely requited his affections by doubting him. 'Tis true it came from the suggestions of that devil Stenwold, and I can scarce bring myself to believe that I would have entertained a doubt of my lord and master if his, to me, inexplicable conduct, when I was rushed away from him on the bluffs above Cockenzie, had not somehow given colour to the suspicion. He sat his horse so quietly, outwardly so indifferent to my appeals; with King James' his purse hanging on the saddle bow, the price of my

dishonour apparently; not even lifting voice, much
less drawing blade or striking blow for me. What
could I think?

Sir Hugh hath often assured me since that he
quite forgives me the suspicion, that he pardons
the anger and resentment I harboured against him,
that it was thoroughly warranted. Being a
woman, albeit according to him a wonder among
women and the best wife a soldier ever had—such
is his fond flattery!—he saith I could not be expected to know what idea was in a mere stupid
man's mind.

And I could not be blamed for not seeing that a
husband at large and free to effect my rescue was
worth a thousand dead ones who had been cut to
pieces by a band of murderous villains before my
very eyes. By which he says he would have effected nothing and perhaps have plunged me into
deeper grief than was mine when I was dragged
away from him.

Besides all this kindness from my lord, I take
some little comfort in the knowledge that my father and Master Dunner also were deceived.
Still they did not love him as I, and I should have
known. Especially as, if I had thought, I would
have known that in no way could my lord have

had any communication with the King since our meeting. But who that is mad with jealousy and fear can think clearly?

I could with more equanimity bear to see him dead rather than dishonoured, as he seemed to me that afternoon when I was ravished away. My fault, my grievous fault, lay in my failure to realise that no power on earth could dishonour my lord. The mere fact that he suffered himself in some degree to be put in this false position, and to answer nothing, ought not at all to have worried me, who, though I knew him but shortly, yet loved him and his greatness of heart so well.

Sir Hugh says, it is nonsense for me to reproach myself for an entirely natural and justifiable thought, but I do; and we Clanranalds—and, although I am only a woman, I have all the pride of race of the stoutest and best of them—have ever loved honour more than life; and my husband's rank, if less exalted than ours, he being but a simple Baronet while we are Belted Earls, is as old and honourable as any one's. After all, I am sure it was that dastardly Stenwold's persistent insinuations—if I may characterise his broad and open remarks about my husband as insinuations—that made all the trouble.

I was so torn between shame and terror and humiliation and fearful anticipation, as I sat in the boat, that I was not mistress of my mind. I was completely in the power of this creature of King James, and my interview with the King at Durham had shown me that defenceless, penniless, helpless, I had nothing good to expect from His Majesty.

I heard the sailors speak of Sunderland, and I knew, therefore, that the King had moved from Durham, perhaps to get out from under the influence of the good Bishop, who had been my champion and advocate, and, in all probability, his chief adviser now would be Lord Jeffreys. God help the man or woman or child subject to his caprice. I knew very well what the King designed for me, but I was quite resolved what to do on that score. I would die without the least hesitation before the King, or any one else, should possess me.

My husband might have been false to me, he might have taken the King's purse, and perhaps be expecting future pay from the King in exchange for me, but I was his wife still and I was a Clanranald, my noble father's daughter,—we were not of the class from whom were chosen mistresses for kings.

I was that desperate and reckless that, if I had or could come at a weapon in my hand when the time came, I was resolved that I would even kill the King myself. I had heard whispers of his courage, or his lack of it rather, and I would gladly kill him rather than submit to his desire, if there was no other way.

It was these desperate resolutions which enabled me to sustain, with some degree of fortitude, my terrible situation. Indeed, my grief was not so much on the score of the future as it was because of the past. The doubt of my husband's love and honour bade fair to kill me. I could take care of myself, and could throw away my life rather than be clasped in any one's arms that had not the right.

Yet I blame myself, with abiding shame; and I still think had I been given opportunity, had Stenwold kept silent, had I been left alone, I might have recovered my faith and trust in my lord, but my captor was constantly at my elbow with his infamous suggestions. Indeed, he played his part well; I knew what he would be at—he wanted to make it easy for the King—but in that effort he failed absolutely. Not even the King himself could do that.

My resentment grew and developed to such an extent that I thought grimly enough that Stenwold might as well introduce a wild animal into the King's closet as to thrust me in there. But I dissembled my feelings to some extent and took care to give my gaoler no faintest hint of my determination.

I was treated civilly enough on the voyage, although Stenwold's every look was an insult, and I felt my heart grow cold under his evil and suggestive scrutiny; yet I knew that I had naught to fear from him. In his mind I was meat for his betters. I was, therefore, under little or no apprehension while on the sea. It was a small ship and wretchedly uncomfortable, but I was a good sailor and, even if I had been a bad one, I should have had too much in mind to have spared thought to anything else, no matter what I might have suffered.

We made rather a quick passage to Sunderland. Indeed, the time seemed frightfully short to me. Anticipating I knew not what, maturing plans involving all sorts of desperate actions in my hard situation, and trying to explain to myself my husband's lack of conduct, I came at last to doubt, and I almost convinced myself that he had not been a party to the outrage. But that conclusion involved me in worse difficulty than before, for it almost forced me to think of him as a coward, afraid to risk his life for my honour, unwilling to die in my defence—God forgive me, my dear husband, that I so wronged you, for cowardice in any man, and especially in the man I honoured with my affection, seemed to me to be the unpardonable sin.

Oh, I was torn, maddened, during that voyage! Married in the morning, separated at noonday—what was in store for me?

It was dusk when we dropped anchor off Sunderland, and my Lord Stenwold had the boat got ready. I followed him into it submissively enough; it was either that or be carried; there was no use in my making a profitless struggle then; I would save my energy and strength for the crucial moment. A leaf out of my husband's book that, had I but known it, which now makes my failure to understand him the more blameworthy in my eyes. I shall never forgive myself for it, although he hath assured me many times that he forgot it, as he forgot everything else that had gone before, in the first kiss he pressed upon my lips in Stenwold House that very night after such exciting hours as I never look for nor want to pass again.

We soon traversed the short distance from the anchorage to the castle. I marked, as we clambered up the bank and took the long walk along the moat edge to bring us to the entrance to the house, which fronted away from the water, that the brigantine got under way and moved over to the Sunderland shore, as soon as the boat rejoined her.

Stenwold House lay on the north, or Monk-wearmouth side, of the river. I surmised that the King had accepted my Lord Stenwold's proffer of his seat near the village so as to be the more private and secluded in his villainy than in the more spacious castle and fort of Sunderland, across the stream.

They had taken my sword from me; my pistols, of course, had been left behind in the holsters attached to my saddle. I was absolutely unarmed and defenceless; I had not even been allowed the privilege of knife and fork on the voyage, my food having been so prepared for me that I could eat it with a spoon.

I had no money; all we possessed, which was but little, being in my husband's keeping, and I had few jewels—a wedding ring and one other.

I did not wish to give up my solitaire diamond, saving it for a last resort, therefore I was without means to bribe; and indeed, in the confines of the small ship, Stenwold kept such close watch upon me that I had no opportunity for speech, even with any one else. Never did I utter such fervent prayers as I did all through that cruise, that God in some way would raise up help for me and enable me to defend that which was dearer to me than life itself—and yet I was young, too, and passionately attached to my husband, and life was sweet.

God was answering my prayers in His own way. Now I thank Him daily for what He did for me and that I enjoy my husband's entire forgiveness and continued love. He blesses me while I write now, who am Sir Hugh's wife, which I find to be so different from what I dreamed it before my marriage. These things do indeed change us more than we wot of, when we give our heart and hand and person into the keeping of some one else. I can scarcely stir without Sir Hugh at my side now; I look to him for everything; his guidance is half my life, his inspiration the rest of it; and I was once the most independent maid in Scotland!

I run on incessantly; there shall be no more in this strain. Suffice it to say that I mounted the great stairs of the castle with a steady step. I was shown through a long hall, then through a smaller room, and then into another, still small but spacious and elegant enough. This room overlooked the water.

Stenwold House was perched on the brow of the cliff, or steep bank, of the Wear. The apartment in which so much took place was in the second story, and perhaps seventy feet from the high-tide line of the river. There was, so far as I could see, but one entrance to the apartment, and that was by the door through which we had come. The room was handsomely furnished, and off to the left through another door, half-opened, I discerned a bed-chamber, at the sight of which I grew cold with fear and shame.

" Will it please you," began my Lord Stenwold, after we two entered the room, and my heart leaped to see that it was empty, " to refresh yourself after your journey? "

" Nothing that you can do or say, or any one else here, will please me in the least degree," I retorted, with what carelessness and firmness I could muster.

" Your ladyship grieves me beyond expression," was his sneering answer. " However, I shall leave the task of pleasing you to an abler and nobler being than my poor self."

" Meaner and baser would be better words, if that were possible," said I.

His face flushed, he glowered at me darkly, he even instinctively touched his sword-hilt.

" Madam, you will live to bless me for this adventure," he said.

" If I live at all, sir," I returned, " I shall curse you to the last day of my life or yours."

" If you would take a fool's advice, madam . . ."

" A knave's rather," I interposed.

" 'Tis much the same thing. We are all of us fools or knaves—some of us both; and the only wise man is he who recognises and admits his knavery or his foolery," he ran on cynically, striving to recover his equanimity.

" You speak capably from your own experience," said I. " I doubt you have met many gentlemen and gentlewomen in your evil life and service, but, if you have, I am sure you have no personal knowledge or experience that would enable you to recognise either."

" Madam, do you know how defenceless you are? " he cried, apparently provoked beyond control by my flings at him. " Do you not know that the King will tire of you as quickly as he fancied you? Do you realise what it would mean to you then, to have a friend in me? "

He approached me threateningly as he spoke.

" I am not so defenceless as you think, Lord Stenwold, and, weak as I am, I have a Friend still who . . ."

" Your husband? " he interposed sneeringly.

" Almighty God," said I.

" God! "

His jaw dropped; I never met such a look of astonishment as I saw in his face, and then he laughed sardonically.

" God may be all right in His heaven, doubtless," he continued, " but we are on earth, and here the King's word rules."

" 'Tis more like hell," I returned.

" And I am devil-in-chief, madam," he said, bowing. " Saving, of course, the King's royal grace and precedence," he added. " But enough of this; His Majesty, I am informed, desires to consult your pleasure in every way. He is kindness itself toward the fair."

" Let him release me then, and restore me to my father."

" In every way but that."

" I have no other pleasure, no other wish, no other will."

" What! not a thought for thy cowardly, treacherous, money-loving husband? "

There he wounded me. I am ashamed to say it, but I thrust my face into my hands and turned away, to hear again that mocking laugh. May God and my husband forgive me, I never can. It was Stenwold who broke the silence that fell between us.

" I shall have something to eat and drink brought to you here. After that, my charge of you is over; I shall deliver you to my royal master."

" May I eat alone? "

" Madam, you may; the taste of your sharp tongue that I have just had hath somewhat impaired my own appetite, I confess. When you are somewhat tamer, I shall visit you again; meanwhile, I wish you joy of your evening, and His Majesty likewise."

There was something ironic in that wish for the King that did give me a certain satisfaction.

I would not give much for any pleasure His Majesty was to get out of me. I thought I was quite capable, in default of other means, of choking the King to death with my own hands, if I could muster the strength, and I believed that in the last extremity I could. I was desperate, you see.

Chapter
XVIII

Wherein Lady Katharine describes what took place in the Antechamber where the King made Love to her

WHILE Stenwold was away, I swiftly examined both rooms—the antechamber and the bedroom: they had no entrance and no exit, save by that one door, which was now locked against me. I had only one resource— I could throw myself from one of the windows to the rocks below as a last resort.

The room was full of light from many candles, the windows were heavily draped; I opened the sash of one of them and fastened it back. Then I drew a chair in front of the open window and covered it with the heavy hangings. The night was fair, there was little or no breeze fortunately. Not enough wind came through the open casement to stir the candles even, or, if there did, the draperies were sufficiently close and heavy to contain it. Without examination, it could not have been known in the room that the window was open or

that the chair was so placed that I could by means
of it leap to the sill.

Fortunately, it was a large window, and I could
throw myself through it in a moment. I did not
want to go to my death yet—I was young, and
loved life, even under the circumstances—and I kept
on hoping against hope. I tried to persuade myself
that there was some explanation of my husband's
conduct that would let me love him and let me
show him that love—I vow before God that I
had not ceased to care for him, in spite of all—
provided I could win away from the dangers I
was in. I would not make the wild plunge until
the last moment.

These hurried inspections and preparations were
scarcely completed when the door was opened, and
Lord Stenwold entered; he was followed by two
lackeys, who brought me a royal repast. It was
set upon a table conveniently placed by direction
of the master of the house, and, when all was in
readiness, he turned to me with a bow and asked
me if there was anything else I wanted. A thought
came to me as I watched them arrange the meal,
and I answered thus:

"Will not my Lord Stenwold, after the watch-
ful care with which he hath looked to me during

our journey, do me the honour to take a glass of wine with me, and drink a toast of my making?"

"My lady, I have never refused to drink, to game, to fight, or to love with anybody on earth," said Stenwold, bowing gallantly, "and I shall not begin now."

"Allow me then."

I stepped to the table, poured out two glasses of wine, proffered him one, and took the other myself. He bowed low as he lifted it up, looking at me inquiringly.

"Your toast, madam?"

"God save the King," said I, with sinister mockery.

I think he must have felt what was in my mind, for that toast was plainly threat, not prayer, and for a moment he hesitated.

"Surely," said I, "no loyal servant of so noble a master can balk at that sentiment."

"So long as you believe in God, madam," he said at last, "you might better have phrased it, 'God save yourself,' but have it your own way; I drink."

I sipped mine; he drained his glass, to my great relief. Then he set the glass down, shrugged his shoulders, turned, and left me. The wine, at least, was not drugged or poisoned. I was not hungry, but I ate heartily for strength and I drank a little of the King's rare vintage, for the same reason.

Again the table provided me with no weapon, yet as I surveyed it disconsolately a thought came to me. I took one of the tall Venetian glasses, went over to the hearth, and deliberately broke it; fortunately, it shattered in such a way as to leave me a smooth space by which to grip it and a sharp edge below to cut or thrust with. It was a poor weapon, but it was the best I could do. I still held it in my hand when again the door was opened; the lackeys removed the table, and as they did so, Stenwold, who had entered again with them, drew aside the heavy curtain veiling the door and said:

"His Majesty the King."

It had come at last, the hour that was to decide my fate, or perchance the King's. Oh, how my heart beat then!

King James entered the room immediately he was announced. Lord Stenwold closed the door, remaining on the outside of it, and I was alone with the King. I had time to mark that the key was not turned and no bolt was shot. That did

me little good, after all, for I realised at once
that Stenwold would keep watch on the other side
and that the whole castle, in fact, would be well
guarded, yet I was glad not to be locked in with
my persecutor.

King James was royally attired, stars and orders like suns blazed on the breast of his coat, he
had all the outward and visible signs of Majesty,
but in his clothing alone; for the rest, his face
was flushed, evidently he had been drinking and
was now perceptibly in his cups, his wig was
slightly awry, his dress disordered—a royal spectacle, indeed! He bowed low before me, where
I stood as cold as the winter's ice, as rigid as one
of our mountains in bonny Scotland, and as dis-
dainful as if he had been the cur that in truth
he was.

" Madam," he said, a little thickly, but with an
evident attempt at amiability, " you are very welcome to our presence. 'Fore God, having seen you
once in that boy's suit, I could not rest until I had
you back again at court."

As he spoke, he looked at me, and the blood
stirred in me from head to foot, following his evil
glances. I could wear that boy's attire before the
world without a thought, but before that King,

not for a second without shame. I had hated him before—I loathed him then.

"I trust," he went on, "that your voyage hither hath been a pleasant one, that your reception hath been commensurate with your beauty, and that your present entertainment is to your liking."

"Your Majesty," said I, "as I told you before in the presence of the good Bishop Ken, who was your good angel on that day . . ."

"Name him not," said the King resentfully; "we are well rid of the pestilent Churchman and his pious advices."

"Not so," I persisted.

"Madam, I will not have him mentioned," growled His Majesty.

"You are, or should be, the font of honour and dignity for these three kingdoms; the oppressed, the weak, the persecuted, the tempted, have only you to whom to appeal, as I, a woman, friendless, alone, bereft of all her protectors, appeal to you now."

"Appeal rather to my love for you, Lady Katharine, and I could deny you nothing," he made answer, smirking odiously at me.

"Rather do I appeal to the King's mercy, the

King's honour, the King's justice . . . !" I cried.

"Mean you Lord Jeffreys?" he asked.

"God forbid!"

"'Twas upon his advice I brought you hither," laughed the Monarch.

"So I might have surmised."

"He told me, in his blunt, rough way, that I was more than a fool to let escape such a delicious little . . ."

"Spare me his vulgar words!" I exclaimed contemptuously.

"I will spare you anything, if you will just love me a little, you little vixen. Come, we have talked enough."

He moved toward me a step. Instantly—God forgive me, it is a fearful thing for a subject to do, but my blood was hot, and I was so enraged— I lifted my hand.

"Come nearer," said I, "and I strike you with this."

The King stared hard at me, and then burst into laughter as he recognised how little formidable a thing it was that I held in my hand.

"What is 't?" he asked. "A bit of broken glass? A woman's weapon."

I was quicker than he thought, for, though he was on me as he spoke and his hand caught at my wrist, I struggled viciously and managed to scratch his face; indeed, I cut it deep enough for blood to come.

" You little spit-fire! " he cried angrily, wresting the broken goblet from me. " What's the matter with you? There is scarce a woman in the realm that would not be honoured by my affection."

" Here is one," answered I, " that finds it only dishonour."

I wrenched myself free from him as he spoke and stepped back from him. He was sober enough now, and in an ugly mood, yet strove to control himself and win me if he could.

" Madam," he pleaded, " be reasonable; you are at my mercy."

" The King's mercy," I mocked. " What mean those words? "

" You don't seem to understand that I love you, Lady Katharine," he went on, " that I can do anything for you, and I will; I will give you riches, I will create you a duchess, I . . ."

" I have already a higher position than any you can give me," I interposed triumphantly.

" And what's that? "

" I am a true and lawful wife."

" Wife to a man who sold you unto me? "

Glad am I—I thank God for it daily; I shall continue so to do so long as I live—that I answered thus:

" That is a lie."

" It is the truth! " cried the King.

" It will take more than the word of James Stewart to make me believe it."

The King laughed.

" You called me James Stewart, Katharine Clanranald."

" Katharine Richmond," I protested.

" Katharine anything you will; I drop my royalty, I cast it aside, I am a man who loves you, who will have you; nay, shrink not back, you are helpless, your reputation is gone already, you might as well have the sweet with the bitter, the reward with the service, and there is no shame in it after all as the world sees it, kings are exalted above other men. Faith, I know not why I plead a moment with you, when I might take you out of hand, but that I . . ."

He stepped toward me; I sprang from him and, being fleeter of foot than he, gained the window before he divined my purpose. I tore away the hangings, I leaped upon the sill, and leaned far out, my right knee upon the sill, my left foot on the chair.

" If you come one step nearer," I cried, looking back at him, " I shall hurl myself upon the rocks below! "

" You wouldn't do that," protested the open-mouthed, astonished King, rooted to the spot where he stood.

" Would I not? If you have the least doubt of my purpose, put me to the test; approach me and I die."

" But I offer you riches, rank, power, my love, everything."

" These things spell but two words for me, James Stewart."

I was resolved that I would no longer call him King or Majesty, who was so unworthy of either title or attributes.

" And what do they spell? "

" Shame—dishonour."

" Hey, woman, would you prefer death to our affection? "

" I would prefer death to your crown, if you went with it! " I cried.

The King's back was toward the door, which was in full view from where I crouched upon the broad window-sill. As he stared at me in bafflement, and as I looked at him in triumph, the door softly opened. I did not care much who came into the room. While I maintained my position, I had my own fate in my own hands if a dozen were beside the King; therefore, I looked with little curiosity and was totally unprepared for what I saw.

Silently a splendid figure came through the slowly opened door, which he quietly closed behind him; in his hand he bore a bloodstained sword. It was my husband! He was true—that was my first thought, I swear.

My heart stopped its beating; unconsciously, I looked away from the King. He had no thought evidently but for me, for, taking advantage of my momentary inattention, in two bounds he was upon me. He laid hold of my ankle, my foot being on the chair, and laughed triumphantly.

But I did not care. I made no effort to throw myself over now, not even did I struggle to release myself; my protector was here. In one second all my trust and confidence came back, so far as he was concerned. I knew he could deal with all

the kings and crowns on earth to save me. I
waited, almost with a sense of amusement at what
I knew would be the instant and appalling discomfiture of the King, who, as he seized me, exclaimed:

" I have you now, madam, and who shall deliver you from my hand? "

" I," said my husband, smiling at me.

Chapter
XIX

Wherein Sir Hugh Richmond interrupts a Tête-à-tête between his Wife and one James Stewart

AND now I resume the telling of my own story. I cannot describe the feeling of thankfulness that filled my heart when I opened the door and saw my wife crouching on the window-seat, and the King standing angry and helpless in the centre of the room. I knew exactly what had been in Lady Katharine's mind: that, rather than submit to the King, she would throw herself from the tower to the rocks below—my brave, beautiful, splendid Kate! I shuddered to think of that catastrophe, and yet I rejoiced that she had found the courage to plan it and that I had come in the nick of time to render it unnecessary.

She saw me so soon as I opened the door. The King's back was toward me, and he was not aware of my presence—he was so intent upon her as to be oblivious to everything else. He observed her gaze, which had been concentrated upon him, I imagined—and she hath since told me it was so—

wander my way for a moment and, with a quickness for which I should not have given him credit,
he realised his opportunity and seized it; for, in
two steps he was by her side, he caught her ankle
in a firm grasp, her foot being on the chair and
her knee upon the window.

Whether he could have effected that or not if I
had not been there, even if her gaze had wan-
dered, I cannot say. His touch was profanation,
but his present actions were of little importance
in my wife's mind or in my own. Since I was
there I had but one course to follow, as ever the
bold one! But, then, I had followed that same
course all along and with success. I had bested
Jeffreys, entered the castle and killed Stenwold,
and I felt no doubt but that I should triumph
over the wretched Monarch, a weaker man than
either of them.

There was, too, a certain grim satisfaction in my
heart in the situation. It is not every day that a
simple soldier and gentleman has the chance to
measure himself against a man who, while he was
not a great King, was, nevertheless, the appointed
ruler over a great realm for the time being.

I had served King James long and well and he
had requited me, after having banished me for a

venial offence that any other monarch had freely pardoned, by endeavouring to take from me all that life held of sweetness and light for me—my bonny Kate, my wife. Had he not laid his hand upon her person, I think I could have waited a little while behind the tapestry enjoying the situation. My wife had ever a witty and a cutting tongue, although she uses it not now upon me—thank God!—and I doubt not that there would have been rare baiting of the King; but the clasp on her dainty ankle and his insulting laugh, his boastful statement, moved me, and I spoke as she hath written.

"Your Majesty," I added quietly, "hath it not been one of the lessons of your kingship that he laughs best who laughs last?"

At the first sound of my voice the King had released Lady Katharine and wheeled to face me. His red face went suddenly white as he saw me standing there, grim, forbidding, with a naked and bloody sword in my hand. I could not have been a very pleasant spectacle, although Lady Katharine, with a woman's fond exaggeration, has since assured me that I was the fairest thing she ever looked upon—for the nonce. I am glad I so appeared to her.

" Holy Virgin! " exclaimed the King, as soon as he could get breath. " Richmond! "

" I am glad to see that Your Majesty recognises me."

" Hugh! " cried my wife, finding voice at last. " Thank God, you have come in time."

" And did you ever doubt that I should be here, sweetheart? " I asked, in turn.

I never took my eyes off the King, though I spoke to her. I stood between him and the door, and, at a move, I could have spitted him like a fowl, and I would, too; I cared not a snap of my finger for his Majesty or his Kingship. By means of the chair, my wife sprang down from the high window and came close to my side, and, before I knew what she would be at, she seized my left hand and kissed it. That sight aroused the King; he opened his mouth to cry for assistance, but, before he could utter a sound, I was upon him fiercely.

" Be silent," I hissed at him, " or I will run you through."

It was impossible for him to turn any whiter, he was so pale already, but he shrank away from the menacing point of the red weapon in terrific agitation.

" You draw your sword against your King? "
he exclaimed.

" You raise your hand against my wife? "
I retorted.

" Down on your knees, sir," said the King,
striving to recover his dominance, " and beg for
your life. Because of your wife, I may give it
to you."

" Now," mocked I, " that is a most royal
clemency on the part of Your Majesty, but, if
any knees press the floor in this room, they will
not be mine."

" I am the King of England . . ."

" No one would ever imagine it from your
actions."

" And you are my subject."

" Nay," said I; " here we be two men—James
Stewart and Hugh Richmond—and of the two I am
the master."

It was about as insulting a thing as I could
say, and the King's position was about as degrading a one as he could well occupy. A moment's
reflection upon it goaded the unhappy man to
madness.

" Stenwold! " he cried out suddenly in a high-
pitched voice.

What more he would have added I do not know, for my sword was at his throat. I even pricked him a little, for I saw a spot of blood stain the lace of his tie. I pressed him hard, too, until he shrank against the wall, helpless.

" Now I am in mind," said I fiercely, " in that you have disobeyed me in calling out, to pin you to the wainscoting and leave you there."

" Would you kill your King? " gasped out James, alarmed beyond measure.

" You are no King of mine," I answered roughly. " For one thing, you have banished me, proscribed me, I am an outlaw, and I would kill you as I would any other rat that came beneath my notice."

" But Stenwold? "

" Would it not otherwise alarm the castle, you might call on Lord Stenwold forever."

" Is he dead? "

" Ay! "

" Did you kill him? "

" Yonder, in the antechamber," I said.

" And you would murder . . ."

" Stop," I interposed. " I killed Lord Stenwold in fair fight."

" But I have no weapon, or . . ." said the

King, eagerly grasping at straws to save the rags and tatters of his self-respect.

And here my wife interposed—she lifted from the chair the jewelled sword which the King had laid aside for his love-making and handed it to him.

" Now you have the means of defence! " I exclaimed, throwing her an approving look for her splendid action and the evidence of her confidence in me.

" I stand here to see fair play," said Lady Katharine fiercely.

I drew back from him a little space to give him room, and fell on guard, but the King's sword hung listlessly from his hand.

" I cannot fight with a subject; 'tis beneath me," he muttered.

" You would fight with a woman, though; you did not find that beneath you," said my wife quickly. " You would contrive to spoil her of that which is infinitely dearer than life. You hesitated not to attempt that."

" But he did not succeed, Kate! " I cried.

" I should be deader than Stenwold then," said my wife.

" If he had, his own life would not be worth

a moment's purchase," said I grimly. " Your conduct passes belief, sir."

" Let us end this comedy," said the King desperately.

" 'Tis not yet decided, sir," I said ironically, " from the first act of the play, whether it shall turn out a comedy or a tragedy."

" You have me in your power," returned James. " What is it you wish? "

" Freedom to depart instantly from this castle with my wife without let or hindrance by you or any one."

" Needs must," said the King. " My hour will come, but this is yours. Go! You are free, but, if you are found within my domains within the hour, God help you."

" Threats," said I mockingly, " ill become the powerless."

" Death and fury! " exclaimed the King, in futile rage.

" And this man presumed to love me," laughed Lady Katharine, " and to think that I could mate with such a coward."

I suppose that was the last straw; the King could stand no more; he tore nervously at the lace of his collar.

"Go!" he cried. "You have my word that you shall not be stopped."

" Your word," I sneered.

" My royal word."

"Your Majesty, it's not worth the breath that utters it. We will have a safe-conduct from Your Majesty in Your Majesty's own hand; we will have Your Majesty's seal to attest the writing lest any question it."

"Anything," said the unhappy King, mad to get us away.

There was a handsome writing-cabinet against the wall.

"Will it please Your Majesty to sit there," said I, pointing with my sword toward the chair before it.

The King actually reeled to the place and fell, rather than sat down, in the seat. He was so agitated he could scarcely hold the pen. I bade him calm himself and take plenty of time, as we were not likely to be interrupted, but my friendly words did not seem to have great effect. He made several ineffectual attempts to write, and finally threw the quill upon the desk.

" Write it yourself," he said, " and I will sign it."

"Nay," replied I, "that can hardly be, for I must keep good watch over you."

"Give me the charge of him, Hugh!" cried my brave Kate eagerly. "You know that I can wield the sword and I have a score of my own to pay back to this man."

"Good," said I.

I passed her my sword, and it pleased my heart to see how firmly she grasped it in her sweet hand, and how like a master she handled it. At the same time I slipped her that little pocket-pistol, of French make, that I carried ever about me in times of hazard.

"Stand up!" she cried abruptly, pointing her blade to the King.

It cut him to the heart to be thus mastered by a woman. He looked at me as if in appeal. I shrugged my shoulders.

"The lady is in command," I said. "I know her well, she's my wife; you had best do as she says, and quickly, or I'll not answer for the consequences."

There was nothing for him but obedience. The unhappy man rose slowly to his feet and stared at us, his eyes distilling hatred.

"Face the wall!" cried Lady Katharine, and

perforce he had to obey again. She rested the sword-point between his shoulder-blades and tapped him lightly therewith.

" Turn but your head, move at all," she said, " and I will run you through." She looked at me for a moment and laughed. " Is it well done, my lord? " she asked.

" Excellent well."

" Behold the Royal Majesty of England! " she laughed. " Flattened against the wall of his own palace and held there at her pleasure and by a woman's hand."

Where have I heard the saying, " Hell hath no fury like a woman scorned "? Well, there was no time for moralising. I sat down, and wrote an order without duress, granting free exit from the castle, without let or hindrance, for Sir Hugh Richmond and Lady Katharine, his wife, with whatsoever jewels and property either bore upon his or her person, and affording them immunity from capture for a space of two hours thereafter. After I had finished it, I sanded it carefully, left it upon the desk and once again resumed my weapons.

" The prisoner, sir," said my wife, with marked gravity, " hath comported himself admirably un-

der our gentle persuasion. He hath not stirred;
yea, he hath scarcely even breathed."

Then laughter overcame her.

" Your Majesty," said I, " you can sign the order now."

The King fell away from the wall and into the
chair, almost like a dead man. He seized the pen
and scrawled his name beneath it with a shaking
hand.

" Now the Royal signet."

His hand trembled so he could scarcely drop
the wax, but at last he managed to affix his seal
to it.

" Leave the seal on the table," I added.

" There it is," he replied, slamming it down
furiously.

" I want to play fair with you," I said. " I
am not a King; you had better read over the paper you have signed."

The King glanced hastily over it and shoved it
toward me.

" Take it, damn you," he said. " If I but get
my hands upon you . . ."

" I know perfectly well what you would fain do
with me," I replied coolly. " And if you catch
me, you have leave, so far as I am concerned, to

wreak whatever majestic vengeance you are inclined to."

" Have you finished this baiting of me now? "
he choked out.

" Not yet. You have confiscated my own estates, also the property of the Earl of Clanranald,
the father of my wife; we paid you ten thousand
pounds for his liberty and for my wife's freedom;
I will take that money, if you please."

" Do you think I carry that much upon my
person? "

" Not in gold or silver perhaps," said I, " but
in the stars and jewels that you wear."

" Wouldst thou rob as well as murder me? "

" I take but my own," returned I. " Off with
them."

The King tore the jewels from his breast, the
rings from his fingers, the pins from his tie, and
heaped them down upon the desk. I gathered them
together and dropped them into my pocket.

" Now," said I, " we have done with you. I
served you long and served you well. My own offence was such as any noble gentleman might have
forgiven; you repaid me by banishment, and then,
ignobly, you tried to steal my wife. True it is
that in old days you did heap benefits upon me;

I requite them by sparing you now; and, with my wife, I go. Understanding that neither your spoken word nor your written pledge is worth much to me, who know you of old, I have here something I fancy which will cause you to respect what you have said and what you have written."

" What is that? "

" Your Chief Devil is locked up and under guard, his life is forfeit for mine."

" Jeffreys! " cried the King.

" Your Majesty hath wit enough to identify him from my meagre description evidently," said I.

" And what of him? "

" He is my prisoner."

" It is a lie."

" I have not rank enough to lie. Here is the evidence."

I forced into his hands Jeffreys' letter.

" 'Tis forged," he protested.

" And is this, too, forged? " I asked, as I showed him my lord's signet ring.

" Does the fool believe," said the King bitterly, " that I would allow his life or anybody's to stand between me and my will? "

As for that, I could quite believe that in his

present mood the King would have sacrificed Jeffreys, or anybody, or anything but his life for revenge upon me and mine, and power to work his
will upon both of us.

"To tell you the truth, sir," I answered
smoothly, "even he does not think that highly of
you, but even Your Majesty could scarcely afford
to have it known that he wilfully sacrificed his
Lord Chief Justice for a woman."

"Enough," said the King; "you have what you
came for; now, go!"

"But one thing more remains to be said," I began. "For the sake of the honourable gentlemen,
the honest and gallant men over whom for yet a
little space you are permitted to rule, and not to
bring shame to them by showing them what a
coward their monarch is, my wife and I will keep
silent concerning the events of this night, and, if
they be mooted abroad, the news will come from
you, not from us. I wish Your Majesty a good-
night."

"Go, go!" cried the King.

"Come, Kate," I said.

I sheathed my sword and then I kissed her before him. I confess I wanted him to see it, that
kiss which he had been denied. Then I took her

hand and we turned happily away. The King sank down into a chair and lay sprawled there, trembling and shaking as if in an ague, while we made toward the door. The desperate game had been played out, and I had won. I was happy, exultant, triumphant. Ten minutes would see us on the water and away, if Macleod had been faithful. which I did not doubt.

Chapter
XX

*How Sir Hugh and Lady Katharine, with some
Assistance from General Feversham, at last and
finally overcame the Majesty of England*

THERE was a sudden clamour in the great
hall outside. My heart stopped beating.
I halted with my left hand on the closed
door. I released my wife and drew my sword
again.

" If anything happens," I whispered to her, " do
you go to the window, dearest Kate! I'll hold
them in play until you leap, and if I can I'll follow
you."

" I understand," she answered, her eyes shining
with love for me and brave determination to die
rather than yield to the King.

A gruff soldier's voice that I recognised said
something I could not make out. The farther door
at which Harkins had kept watch was suddenly
thrown open. Through the closed door between
the King's chamber and the anteroom where dead
Stenwold lay I could hear confused noises, clashing

of arms, many people entering hurriedly, then that deeper foreign voice, that I knew but could not place, commanded silence. The King had heard as well as I.

" 'Tis Feversham," he exclaimed, leaping to his feet, his face changing. " We shall see now who wins."

As he spoke another harsher, rougher voice came through the door.

" And Jeffreys! " cried the delighted King. " Down on your knees, you dog," he roared. " He doth laugh best who laughs last. Madam, you did ill to trust yourself to this man."

I stood appalled for the moment at this sudden check to our plans.

" Gentlemen, to me," roared the King. There was a surge toward the door, which had been thrown open at the King's first shout for assistance, and in the instant the room was filled with men. But I was quicker than any. I stepped to the side of the King and dragged him back to the wall near the window before he himself or any one else could prevent. My wife followed me.

" Your Majesty," I said quickly, while the newcomers stood surprised beyond measure, " I have you covered, have a care what you do. My life is forfeit, but if I die, you die before me, dost understand?"

At that second Feversham and Jeffreys in the lead, the officers of the guard following, with the King's gentlemen and Stenwold's lackeys, all stepped toward me. The King and I stood together near the middle of the wall of the farther room, Lady Katharine alone near the window adjoining us.

"Back," cried the wretched King, desperately urged thereto by the pressure of that small pistol against his back.

"Your Majesty . . ." began Feversham, stopping short, and then he recognised me. "Richmond!" he exclaimed; "Lady Katharine Clanranald!"

"Katharine Richmond, sir," protested she, proud of her new name.

"You came in the very nick of time, Lord Feversham," said the King. "Sir Hugh Richmond is a traitor and an exile, he is an outlaw, he hath raised his hand against his King, as you see. Take him: We will decide upon his punishment later."

"Ay, Your Majesty, and if that be not enough, he tied me up, like a trussed fowl, threatened me with death, and left me two hours since with a dirty rag in my mouth. But for the chance arrival at the inn of Lord Feversham, who insisted upon seeing me when he heard I was there, I might have died of thirst or suffocation," roared out Jeffreys.

"He hath killed my Lord Stenwold," cried another.

"'Fore God, let's burn the dog, and——"

"Lord Feversham," cried my wife in swift interruption. "You served me well once in my need, hear me now. In violation of his honour, the King employed Lord Stenwold to bring me here against my will, to my shame, for His Majesty's foul purpose."

"Silence, wench," roared the King.

But I shoved my pistol harder into his side.

"Give the lady free speech," I said grimly, "and do not use that word again to my wife if you love life."

"And my husband came here in the nick of time to rescue me from His Majesty——"

"And to avenge you had I been too late," I added.

"What man of you would not do the same, for one he loved?" she cried, appealing to the rest.

"You, Lord Feversham, are a French gentleman, one of the *haute noblesse* of your gallant land, an honourable soldier; what say you? Is my husband to be blamed for that? Is his life to be forfeit because he sought to protect me from this dishonoured King?"

Never had she been so royally beautiful herself as in that hour. I knew not till then how fortunate I had been in winning her to wife. I almost forgot our lives hung upon her word in admiration for her, but nevertheless I kept tight hold of the King.

Louis de Duras looked greatly troubled.

"Your Majesty," he said at last, "deny this for God's love, and for the sake of your kingly fame!"

"Why should I deny it?" snarled the King. "The woman is my subject, the daughter of one traitor, the wife of another—she ought to be honoured."

"It is ill done, Sire," said the soldier, shaking his head.

"The King can do no wrong," roared Judge Jeffreys.

"I should have left you where I found you by chance," said Feversham, looking contemptuously

at the red-faced travesty of justice, " the soiled
rag thrust within your lips consorts well with what
falls from them now and ever."

" Lord Feversham," cried the King, as Jeffreys
shrank away from the fierce gaze of the proud,
brave soldier, " on your allegiance I command
you to obey my order."

" One step nearer, General Feversham," cried I,
tapping the King on the shoulder—he was as a
child in my hands!—" and I blow His Majesty's
brains out before you all."

" Would you murder your King? " cried Jeffreys.

" Ay, and die regretting that I had not a second
shot for you."

Feversham stood uncertain. Jeffreys gnashed
his teeth in baffled rage and terror.

" Good God, gentlemen! " protested the Lord
Chief Justice, " is all the power of England in
this vagabond's hands? "

How the situation might have terminated I cannot say. We had reached a position in which advance or retreat were alike impossible on either
side. It was my bonny Kate who intervened
again. God bless her woman's wit. It saved us
both. She suddenly stepped past the Earl of

Feversham toward me. The soldier bowed, but made as if he would interrupt her progress.

" Madam," he said, " I respect you, but I must guard as I may the person of the King; your husband alone sufficiently menaces him. What want you now? "

" Sir," said my wife, looking him full in the face, " I give you my word of honour, as the daughter of the Earl of Clanranald, as the wife of Sir Hugh Richmond, for we were married three days ago in Scotland, that I mean no harm to the King, although he hath threatened me with much. I only wish to take from the person of my husband, he being otherwise occupied and so unable to hand it to me, a paper and a seal for your inspection."

" Keep the woman back, Louis," began the King imploringly, but I thrust him savagely with the muzzle of my pistol and his voice died away.

" Madam, I take your word," said Feversham, bowing gallantly. " Pass on."

" By God! " exclaimed Jeffreys, " if you would let me deal with the woman, we'd have His Majesty freed from that knave in a moment. We could have held her as hostage, man."

The King looked gratefully, the General scornfully at Jeffreys, who certainly had spoken shrewdly if too late.

At that moment it repented me that I had not killed him when I had the chance. It was however now impossible to carry out his suggestion, even if Feversham had been so minded. My wife stood close to me and reached her hand into my breast pocket where I had thrust them, and drew forth the King's letter and the King's seal; in three steps she was by Feversham's side, showing by her approach a confidence in him that touched him evidently, and laid the paper in his open hand.

" What's this? " asked the General.

" Read, sir," answered Lady Katharine.

He stepped nearer the light and opened the document.

" 'Tis a free passage and immunity for Sir Hugh Richmond and his wife, given without duress and signed by the King," he said.

" This ring, you know it? " continued my wife.

" The King's seal," answered Feversham. " Your Majesty, did you issue this pass? "

" Yes," said the King, " but——"

" Pardon me, Your Majesty," said I, pressing him a little harder in the back, " you gave me the document of your own free will, did you not? "

"Yes, that is——" stammered the poor King, his face sweat-covered.

"There hath been no one here could put any compulsion upon Your Majesty, hath there?" I asked, ruthlessly pressing my advantage.

"No," he stammered out at last, "but I will revoke the pass."

"'Tis too late," said Feversham bluntly, "unless by a written order."

"And at this moment," said I grimly, "the King cannot write."

"Good God, Feversham!" began the King, but he got no further.

"This is monstrous!" cried my Lord Chief Justice.

Feversham fiercely turned on him as a dog upon a rat.

"This is a military matter," he roared. "Will you be silent? Sir Hugh Richmond, you and your wife by the King's written order are entitled to free passage; as loyal subjects of His Majesty, we respect his name and seal. Back, gentlemen. Way for Sir Hugh and Lady Richmond."

"Gentlemen," said I, "a word before we go. "Lord Stenwold lies dead in yonder chamber, 'tis true, but it was in fair fight. I am this night for the Low Countries; if any friend of his wishes satisfaction and fancies himself aggrieved, I shall hold myself at his disposal in Holland, upon whatever terms he will."

" I shall see," said Feversham gravely, " that your courteous offer be communicated to whomsoever may desire to take up the late Lord Stenwold's quarrel."

" Thank you," said I. " We are indebted to you for much."

" A word before you go," said Feversham. " You know that I had no hand in bringing your wife back here."

" I never for a moment dreamed of it," I replied with a black glance at Jeffreys, who shrank away. " I know well whence the King's evil inspiration came."

" It grieves me," continued Feversham, " to call attention to the fact that if within two hours you are apprehended on English ground, your life, and I doubt not," he added significantly, " your wife's honour will be forfeited."

" I understand," said I. " Your Majesty," I turned and faced the King. I took off my hat and bowed low to him with ironic courtesy—indeed had he not sought to use me and mine so foully,

I could have pitied him in his degradation and despair—" Good-night, again; you should sleep sweeter for the failure of your designs upon this lady. I trust that I may meet you upon some wider field than this narrow room, where the prize to be struggled for may not be a woman's honour, but a kingdom's rule."

I clapped my hat on my head, drew my wife's hand through my left arm and, with my bare blade in my right hand, I walked proudly through the door. The gentlemen and soldiers assembled silently gave back and opened way by General Feversham's directions as we passed through them. The King and Jeffreys both opened their mouths in wild clamour, but Feversham was equal to the emergency, he roared out like a stentor:

" The King and his Chief Justice would fain be alone, gentlemen. Let us leave the room immediately. Stand not upon the order of your going, sirs——"

And so bellowing orders and commands drowning out the sharp words of the King, he hustled all of them out into the anteroom, closed the door and himself stood guard before it. No one could pass then.

" For God's sake, make haste, Richmond! " he

cried, as I looked back to catch one last glimpse
of him splendidly barring the King's exit.

For the second time that night King James was
a prisoner. I had no fear for Feversham, the best,
the only commander worthy the name in the kingdom; he was a soldier; the King might hate him
but he could do nothing, especially as any indignity
to the Earl would probably cost him the favour of
and might involve him in a war with France, which
at that unsettled time would have been fatal to his
kingship. He needed him.

At the door old Harkins waited; he had posted
himself there, and there he intended to wait whatever came. His face was white enough under its
tan. As I passed by he presented arms and looked
intently at me.

"You are to come with me," I said, assuming
an authority I did not have.

He followed me without a question. We
marched rapidly down the long hall, only to be
halted at the further end by the officer of the
guard; but here another officer overtook us, having been despatched by Feversham, and ordered
that we be given free passage.

The officer looked sharply at the sergeant but
said nothing; fortunately he was but a young

soldier, and I suppose he thought that Harkins was only discharging his duty by escorting me on my way. So the four of us marched down the stair, through the hall, across the courtyard and outside the gates. Here the officer halted.

" I would best see them safe across the draw-bridge and down the road, sir," said Harkins gruffly.

" Very good; go on," said the officer indifferently, turning back.

In half a dozen steps we were over the draw-bridge, and in another moment the three of us were running madly toward the river bank. Harkins' presence was invaluable now, for he knew a path to the water's edge. We fell rather than climbed down it in the darkness and stood knee-deep in the river.

" Macleod! " I cried anxiously.

" Here, your honour, and thank God," came to us out of the darkness, and presently guided by our voices, the prow of a comfortable wherry ran against the bank of the river.

I lifted Lady Katharine into the boat, clambered into the stern sheets myself and seized the tiller, while Harkins sat down forward of Macleod and finding another pair of oars broke them out, and the two men rowed us away from the castle toward the mouth of the river.

Evidently Clanranald's impatience had become so great that he could not remain at sea, for the vessel, with the three lights still twinkling like stars of hope in the blackness, had ventured into the river and was near at hand. I sat in the stern-sheets of the boat, Katharine was next to me, my arm about her, her head upon my shoulder.

The men rowed lustily and in half an hour we were at the ship's side, in five minutes more Katharine was clasped in Clanranald's arms, the wherry was turned adrift, the ship's head was cast off shore, the sails were sheeted home, and we bore away for Holland and Prince William's court—for happiness, for love, for freedom.

Ere we went below into the comfortable cabin to tell the Earl our story, I was stopped by dame Alison and Macleod.

" Lord Stenwold, sir? " asked the former.

" Dame Alison," said I, " he will kiss no more women this side of hell, for he lies dead in his own castle by my own hand."

" That is well done, sir," said Macleod heartily. " Thank you and good-night."

He touched his bonnet, turned and, followed by

his wife, disappeared. Lady Katharine was standing in the light that broke from the cabin door looking toward me. I was very happy, very thankful. I took off my own hat in turn, looked up to the stars, and made a brief soldier's prayer before I followed her into the cabin.

" I thank Thee too, O Lord, and good-night ! "

THE END